CRAZY SH*T IN ASIA

CRAZY SH*T IN ASIA

WHAT COULD GO WRONG?

MATT TOWNER

NEW
HOLLAND

CONTENTS

INTRODUCTION

The idea for this series of books is not just to celebrate alternative travel culture and to keep the dream alive but also to encourage a new generation of travelers and writers to put down their phones and explore the world. In fact, go to places where phones do not work; these are often the places where you learn the most.

My first anthology of adventure travel stories, I had titled 'Travelers' Tales' because that is exactly what they are, adventure travel stories with a sense of humor. My wise and wonderful international publishers headlined the first book *Abroad, Broke & Busted* and stories in that book took readers on journeys which ended anywhere from jails to hospitals, castles to jungles. That first book introduced a new audience to writers as young as teenager Storm Gray through to veteran travel writer Kevin Moloney, amazing female writers like Veronica Farmer, through to learned scholars like Nick Taylor. The book had a little bit of everything and opened the cockpit for us to fly on to a whole series of books.

This time round, our publishers insisted that the stories we tell, and in fact the lives we live, are CRAZY SH*T! At first, I was taken aback. As alternative as I may be and as wild a life as I may live, my mother would be horrified to think that there would be any swearing in my books at all, let alone that the title of the series would be CRAZY SH*T. But as I slept on it, I realized that those words and those words alone, not only explain perfectly my life but also the lives of my fellow adventure travel writers.

We are on a constant quest to uncover the unknown. Not just in terms of people and places but also finding those far out places within ourselves, our minds, our desires, our hopes and dreams. Following in the footsteps of Jack Kerouac, Hunter S Thompson, Timothy Leary, Terrence McKenna and others who traveled not just physically and geographically but mentally and spiritually; pushing the bounds of reality, of what is real and not real, what is normal and what is crazy. I have always said that I learnt more in my first year of traveling than I did in three years of university. I left Australia as a private school boy rugby player with a film and media degree, and 12 months later I was a gem dealing gypsy. This will be the title of my next book, as requested by my publishers in chief.

Like many of the writers in this book, my travels began in those times BC (before computers) but the adventures have never stopped. Our stories are both a celebration of those times as well as a welcoming, and sometimes a warning for those worldly wanderers just heading off now to discover new experiences. When I first left Australia, my father's good friend gifted me a book titled *The Life and Crimes of Charles Sobhraj* written by award winning journalist, the late Richard Neville. Sobhraj was a gem dealer who lived in Bangkok who was incredibly charismatic and had a way with people that drew them to him. I had no idea as I read the book, flying to

San Diego to play rugby for a season, that two years later I would be doing exactly that. But unlike me, and in fact the total opposite, Charles Sobhraj was a serial killer who preyed on travelers. That book taught me from my first international flight that one must be very aware of anyone you meet on the road around the world. I hope that our stories not only entertain and excite but also save someone from making some of the same mistakes we may have made.

Crazy sh*t can be fun and often is, but care is important and knowledge is key. Street smarts come into their own when traveling, especially in those days before the internet. But even now, in the maze of TripAdvisor and Instagram, friends and followers, nothing has changed, in that you really need to know people or places before you can trust them completely. I hope that you will enjoy our stories but also that they move you in some way, whether that be laughter or tears, fear or foresight, because all of those things are what adventure travel is all about and that is Crazy Sh*t.

Matt Towner

CHAPTER 1

ANJUNA MARKETS

Megan Jennaway

The bus station is frantic. Buses whirl in and out of bays like Kandian dancers. No sooner are passengers debouched onto the dirt than the buses fill up again like submerged canoes. Pondo! Quepem! Margao! Santoz! intone the conductors. They roam the queues, transacting destinations like stakes in a lottery.

A woman squats on a kerb behind trays of oranges, stacked in a pyramid. She beckons me over. I shake my head; this is no time for oranges. A gold ring waggles in her left nostril as she leans forward. She cuts open an orange for me to sample. No, I say, *nahin*. I have lost my party. I must find them.

Already I'm regretting the decision to bring our packs. I lumber along under the weight of mine, colliding with small boys and tripping over mangy dogs. Having the packs with us means we won't have to go back to Colva tonight.

Monica! Looking up I see Rob calling out to me from the window of a bus. My heart lurches – will it wait for me? Awkwardly, I try to run, my backpack slowing me down. Scores of heads pop out of windows as I pass, hugely entertained. By the time I arrive the bus has already started to move. With an unnecessary excess of body contact, the conductor hauls me up the steps. Flushing angrily, I slide my pack off my shoulders. The bus is already moving as I stack it next to the others' in the space behind the driver.

Rob surrenders his window seat to me. I ask him how he knows that this is the Anjuna bus. He says they heard a conductor say so, back at the station.

The bus is only mildly overcrowded. Across the aisle, a woman wipes her baby's vomit with the tail of her sari. Two more children are wedged in beside her, crushing an older girl up against the window.

I'm grateful for the little sacrosanct space around me, the buffer Rob provides between me and all the other passengers. It's possible to enjoy traveling in India when you have such a privilege, a little shell of privacy and a window onto the world.

I feast my eyes on the cane fields scrolling past. The sprawling mango trees and thick clumps of bamboo are reminiscent of home. Except that you don't see these graceful adobe cottages around the north coast New South Wales, Australia, their tiled roofs and painted shutters proclaiming a Portuguese past. Under the low arch of almost every stone porch, one or several males can be seen lounging against the balustrade, drinking feni.

More Kerala ganja. For the seventh time today, I decline the reefer in Rob's hand. I prefer not to be giggling when negotiating India's public spaces; events may quickly take a bizarre turn. Rob passes the joint back to Mark and Alison, in the front seat. They've been stoned all morning, trying to tranquillize their mounting impatience.

This is our last chance to get to Anjuna Markets. They only come around once a week, and we've missed two already – thwarted by the shellfish Rob was given one morning in return for helping pull in the nets. The fresh crabs and shrimp had to be cooked then and there, in ashes, with the sparkling ocean, clear sunshine, and the inexhaustible river of ganja on hand. The second time I had period pain. Tomorrow I leave for Mysore, and Rob will probably tag along with me.

Perihan and Wolfgang are moving north to Arambol, reputed to be less of a rip-off than Colva. Joe and Mark and Alison will probably head off elsewhere too, they say, although perhaps not. They've been going to leave for the past six months, but somehow, they always end up staying on.

Perihan is sitting beside Wolfgang, in the aisle across from Mark and Alison. Joe is somewhere down the back. The children of the mother with the vomiting baby are pulling Perihan's hair. The crosser she gets, the funnier they think it is. They hide their faces in their arms and giggle.

Perihan asks me the time again. She does not normally approve of watches in India – we are not mindless instruments of capitalism out here, are we? – but this morning she has asked me every five minutes. She was not amused when I started going backwards: 11.15, 11.05, 10.58. This time I answer, truthfully, that it's 12.35.

It seems like we'll never get to Anjuna. It's taken us nearly six hours to get this far. We tried to get off to an early start this morning, rising at seven. Then Wolfgang discovered he had left his kerosene stove behind. While he went off to retrieve it, everyone else discovered they were hungry. We settled in at the Sunrise Cafe and devoured lassi and pancakes. Then Joe had an imperative urge to hear, one last time, the Bowie album that is listed on the menu as 'Murky Dory'. Two glasses of chai later, nothing had happened. Joe chased up the little boys who wait on us, only to be told that the cassette deck was out of order. They knew that when he first asked, but didn't want to disappoint him by telling the truth. At that point we left, reaching the bus station just in time to see our bus pulling out.

It took us another hour to get to Margao. From Margao, there are buses to Panjim, and from Panjim, buses to Anjuna. But we missed our connection to Panjim, because Mark wanted to check poste restante in Margao one last time. There was nothing for him, of course; fretting over money, he had checked it only the day before.

So, because of Mark's elusive social security check, a kerosene stove and a broken cassette deck, we did not reach Panjim until midday. Even then we came close to missing our Anjuna connection, because of my bladder and a woman selling oranges.

Already it seems as though we've been traveling all day. We're all anxious to see Anjuna now, with its fabled markets. Rob, Wolfgang and Perihan have been to them before, on previous trips to India. That they keep coming back must mean something. In the two weeks we've all been hanging out together, not a day has gone past without somebody referring to Anjuna Markets. For instance, Perihan might say to me, having examined my silver belt from Jodhpur, that it is nearly as fine a quality as the ones you can get from the silver merchant at Anjuna Markets. Whenever the nights have been cool enough for her to bring out her soft Kulu shawl, she's repeated the tale of how she bargained with the Tibetan trader there for three whole hours to get the price down. And several times, with all of us sitting around the campfire, Wolfgang has been persuaded to bring out the collection of precious amethysts, sapphires, pink coral, turquoise and carnelian that he hopes to sell to the assorted freaks, hippies and drug dealers who preside over this legendary bazaar.

At night my mind has been awash with visions of Nepali traders plying yak-hair waistcoats and hand-painted thankas, and Gujarati women selling heavy cotton skirts embroidered with mirrors; of magic Baluchi rugs from Samarkand, and wild Mongolian horsemen playing polo. I've dreamed of misty moonlight fairs beside Lake Pushkar, of caravans plying the Silk Road and nomads with swinging plaits blowing their horns across the empty steppes. Rob laughs at my dreams, saying I am more likely to run into a familiar face from the markets at home than Genghis Khan.

Mark is asking Rob whether the Music House is still in operation. Rob says he thinks so, although it's been much harder for the German band to cart their gear across from Europe since the revolution in Iran. He's heard that they ship it via Bombay now. I ask if they bring their own PAs and amplifiers over from Europe. Of course, says Rob. How else would they get such a good sound? They rent the Music House for a pittance, he tells us, which allows them to stay on and play music for the entire season.

It's a non-stop party, adds Mark, although it really peaks after a market day, especially if it coincides with a full moon. It doesn't take much, he says, for the band to throw another party. It's what they do.

Perihan is slapping the hands of the children behind her. She is the daughter of a Turkish politician and has a low aggravation threshold. The mother looks on in surprise.

Hours go by like towns or landforms, as though time is impregnated into the terrain. I'd almost be content to sit here gazing out across rice paddies and cane fields forever if it weren't for the lure of the markets. The others, though, are visibly restless – Wolfgang and Perihan bickering over whether Wolfgang's broken sandals can be fixed by the simple expedient of a new buckle, or whether he needs a whole new pair. Alison is humming Bob Marley to herself, the way she does when she's nervous. Mark is fishing out the little plastic sandwich bag in which he keeps his ganja – I can tell by all the rustling. Beside me, Rob lengthens and contracts his neck like a heron, trying to work out where we are.

Suddenly the bus lurches left, sending our packs sliding across the floor. We've left the highway. The road before us is wide and pretty, lined with shops and taverns all the way down to the beach. Outside a small cafe-bar we come to an abrupt stop. The driver cuts the engine.

I ask Rob if this is Anjuna. He replies no, he thinks it's Calangute. Already people are clambering out over our packs, the driver among them. I assume he is stopping for a piss or a bidi. He disappears into the bar.

By now we are the only people left on the bus. Perihan checks with Rob: this is not Anjuna, is it? Wolfgang says, maybe the conductor at Panjim was wrong. He goes outside to look at the sign on the front of the bus.

It is clear by now that the bus driver has no intention of returning. Everybody is in a jitter. Wolfgang reappears. The sign says 'Anjuna', he tells us.

Perihan is not one to suffer inconvenience lightly. The little tic which she often gets on the left of her now-compressed upper lip has reappeared. 'Wait here everyone,' she instructs us. 'I'm off to find the driver.'

From the large windows of the bus we observe her diminutive form striding out across the street and into the bar. Moments later, she re-emerges, bandy-legged driver in tow, dragging him by the wrist to a neutral place in the front courtyard. A bidi droops from the corner of his mouth; he is bewildered by this explosive tom thumb of a woman in front of him. The windows are partially open; we can hear their conversation from the bus.

'You must take us to Anjuna now,' she demands. 'We are late for the markets.'

'This no Anjuna bus,' he replies defensively.

'Yes, it is,' she insists, 'it says so out the front. In any case, we've paid to go all the way to Anjuna.'

'Price no different,' he responds cannily. 'This no Anjuna bus, Calangute only. That one Anjuna.' With a sweep of his hand he gestures down the road towards the unlikely prospect of the sea.

The others begin to collect their luggage and leave the bus – the heat must be inclining them to fatalism. One by one, they trickle off down the dusty road, leaving me to wait for Perihan. Eventually I concede that she could be some time. While she continues to harangue the driver, I maneuver both our packs down the steps.

Perihan does not surrender easily. She's the only person I know who will walk 3 kilometers in the steaming heat to save 50 paise (about five cents) on the price of chai between one cafe and another. For Perihan, it's a matter of honor not to be ripped off. She never pays 'tourist price' for anything – it sets a bad precedent. For the same reason, she detests my practice of giving money to beggars. Precedent or not, imagine if we all gave something, I argue, redistributing the wealth downwards. She snorts at me – Christian claptrap. Beggar mothers often break the legs of their children, she says, just to appeal to sentimental people like me. Maybe if we all gave money they wouldn't have to, I reply. Perihan returns, furious. The driver will not accede. He is a very rude man, she tells me, as I help her shoulder her pack.

We catch up with the others in the square down the road. No bus in sight. Joe's already made preliminary inquiries: there are no more buses to Anjuna today. All of them left earlier this morning and will stay out there all day to bring the marketgoers home again. Rob is staring at a bus timetable as though if he stares at it long enough he'll conjure up a bus. Mark and Alison have drifted off. Joe tells me they're thinking of walking the five miles to Anjuna via the beach.

Perihan suggests hitchhiking. But Wolfgang's thirst is more pressing. He wanders over to the cafe facing the square, and we straggle along behind, like a string of rusty cowbells.

In the cool of the cafe courtyard we order 7-Up and freshly-squeezed lemon water and discuss our options. Everyone agrees that hitching is our only alternative, but we're stupefied now with heat and buses. No-one can be bothered to move.

I notice that a man is watching us from another table. There's something anomalous about him. His black eyes and dark skin are Eastern, but he wears an embroidered waistcoat over cotton drawstring pants like a hippie. His hair pokes out from under his pillbox cap, stiff and jet-black. I see wild Mongol horsemen before my eyes.

Perihan cannot contain her impatience. She stamps her foot at Wolfgang. 'Are you finished?' she demands, 'because if we don't get to the markets soon it won't be worth going.'

Everyone looks embarrassed, wondering whether we are all included in the rebuke. Suddenly I realize that the cluster of Ambassadors in the square are taxis. I've been staring straight at them all this time. Why not get a taxi? I suggest. Everybody is stunned by the obviousness of the solution, until Wolfgang points out that they don't have much room. He's right. Ambassadors are modeled on the design of a 1950s Morris Oxford. They seat five people comfortably, six at a pinch. It's only for 5 miles, I reply. I go outside to negotiate a price.

In a dimly-lit tavern across the road I locate a small-boned man in flares and platform shoes who identifies himself as a taxi driver. He talks nervously, trying to flatten his side-parted, wavy hair with his hand. Perhaps he is embarrassed on my behalf, perhaps a woman is not supposed to enter a bar like this, or perhaps it is some more subtle code that I am breaking, like addressing him directly. He gives me a quote of five rupees per head. I ask him to wait.

Back in the cafe, I see that Mark and Alison have returned. I did not account for them in my negotiations with the cab driver. They've decided not to walk to Anjuna after all, they're going to come with us instead. I go back across the road to get a revised quote. It is still five rupees each.

'But that's a rip-off!' exclaims Perihan, when I return. Together we go back out to the taxi driver, still stranded under the tree where I first left him, awaiting our verdict.

Perihan insists we should all pay less because there's two extra passengers. The driver baulks. 'What difference does it make to you whether there's five or seven passengers,' she demands, 'you'll still get your money.'

He disputes the point with her. 'Five passengers are the legal limit,' he says. 'If I take seven, polisi come. So, you must all pay.' He makes a gesture that suggests handcuffing.

He has a point. If the other two don't pay him why should he take the extra risk? But Perihan's outrage is undiminished. 'You are just trying to rip us off,' she accuses him. 'You want to steal money from tourists. You're despicable!'

The driver has not understood a word. He just sees a vitriolic little person standing in front of him, stamping her foot. I can tell from his face that he's thinking about returning to the cool of his bar, where he can drink his feni in peace and quiet, far from the histrionics of foreigners.

Returning to the cafe, we find the anomalous man has joined our table. Qasim has offered us all a lift to Anjuna, Rob announces cheerfully. He owns the 1963 Dodge utility parked outside and we should all fit easily into the back.

Qasim is from Afghanistan. He has been living in India since the Soviet invasion. He offers around a packet of Camels. Rob and Joe each take a cigarette.

'I would like to go back to help my country,' Qasim tells us, 'to fight with the Mujahideen. But mine uncle tells me it is not possible; mine country needs me here in India. We have very important work here in India,' he says, dropping his voice. 'Top secret.'

I am riveted. I want him to tell me more about Afghanistan. Rob wants to know more about his work here in India. Lowering his voice even further Qasim asks Rob, you smoke hashish?

Immediately Mark and Joe lean forward, all ears. Alison hums Bob Marley to herself. Perihan is sulking. I listen to Qasim's patter. 'I have good Afghani black,' he is saying. 'Very best quality, from Mazar-i-Sharif.' He unfolds a small parcel from a waistcoat pocket. 'Look,' he croons, like a gem merchant dazzling his customers with rubies. 'Very smooth, very fresh, no dry like Nepal.'

'Is that all you've got?' asks Mark, unimpressed by the two ounces. Qasim waves his hand airily towards the Dodge. 'Me have more in car. Much more. In glove box. For selling, Anjuna Markets. I show you.'

'Wolfgang,' screams Perihan, 'I'm going! Are you coming or not?'

Qasim looks up, startled. The drinks he has ordered for us have just arrived. The waiter unloads them onto the table. You go Anjuna now? Qasim asks Perihan, his dark eyes flashing. Okay. I take you. He stands up and calls for the bill. We all rise with him, sensing his anger. Rob tries to help him pay, which only angers him more. We have transgressed something, a thin line. We leave our drinks untouched on the table.

Once outside, Rob and I take the front seat with Qasim; the others pile into the back with our packs.

Still agitated, Qasim fidgets with the keys. No-one speaks. Finally, he slots them into the ignition and starts the engine. There are many more people out on the street now, I notice, as Qasim does a U-turn and takes off down the road. Siesta must be over. For several minutes I'm hypnotized at the people scattering before the windscreen, like moths or insects, until I realize that this means we're traveling way too fast. I look across to Qasim's speedo. It

21

doesn't work but his still-irate face tells me all I need to know. Rob and I exchange perturbed glances. Up ahead, a stationary taxi at an intersection is about to make a right turn. Without slowing, we swerve left to avoid it. Our perception gradually dilates as we register a slight impact: a bicycle mounting the left fender. It spurts upwards, somersaulting slowly into the air before diving back down to the ground. As we come to a halt my ears are ringing. We have hit a little boy.

Releasing ourselves from the cab, Rob and I go straight over to the child. He lies bleeding in the dirt, trapped underneath his bike. He has gashes to his face and chest and his leg, tangled up in the wheel spokes, is spouting blood.

A crowd has formed around us. Can someone fetch a doctor, or an ambulance? I try to hide the panic in my voice. The crowd looks back at me blankly. Is there any water? I shriek. Can someone bring water, '*Pani? Pani?*'

This is not a Hindi-speaking area, but I sense movement. Some children are dispatched. The crowd continues to stare at me, as though brained by lightning. Rob rolls a towel from his pack underneath the child's head. Carefully, we extricate him from beneath the bike. We have difficulty with the leg though. There's blood everywhere and we can't see what we're doing. In the end Rob cuts some of the bicycle spokes with his army knife and we disentangle his limb.

I wonder where the child's mother is, whether his brothers and sisters are in the crowd. At last the water arrives. Tearing a strip of cloth off my skirt, I bathe the wounds, binding the leg securely. I watch as the green cotton strip slowly turns pink. Ripping another strip from my dress, I bind it again, and again, until the flow eases.

There's still no reaction from the boy, even though it must be painful. Rob takes his pulse; still strong. 'He must be concussed,' I say. Rob makes a grim face. We wait for the doctor. No sign of Qasim or Joe, nor Mark or Alison. No sign either of Perihan or Wolfgang. I put them out of my mind, everything reduced to this pinpoint vision – a badly-injured child, blood and bike spokes, a throng of onlookers.

The late afternoon pours a sickly yellow light over everything. Still we await the doctor. Cadaverous faces form a cordon around us. We wait. No-one comes. We wait. And wait. The sun slips lower in the sky.

At last someone comes. Not the doctor, not Qasim, but a couple of policemen. They want to know who the owner of the vehicle is. They need registration papers, passports. We appeal for their help, point to the child. They ignore us. Who owns the truck? We say it belongs to an Afghan refugee who has just this minute disappeared. One policeman takes notes. The other narrows his eyes at us. He asks to see Qasim's bona fides. We say we have no idea where he keeps them. Rob offers to check the car. The policeman with the narrowed eyes suggests checking the glove box and offers to accompany him. Rob hesitates, thinking of the hash. But he is committed now. Together they search the glove box. No hash. No papers either.

The police think Qasim is an invention. They demand to see our passports.

Joe reappears. Not realizing an interrogation is taking place, he squats down beside us, convivial. Mark and Alison have gone off to cut hash with Qasim, he informs us, and last he saw Perihan and Wolfgang, they were getting into a taxi. Belatedly, he notices the police, the wounded child. What's happening here? he asks.

The police don't like our whispering. They think we are plotting something. They tell us we are under arrest. Then the doctor arrives, wriggling his way through the crowd.

The doctor is a little fat man with a briefcase. He kneels down beside the boy, apologizing to us. He presses a stethoscope to the boy's chest, opens and closes the boy's eyelids. 'Oh my goodness,' he keeps saying. 'This boy is having a very serious injury.'

'Will he live?' I ask.

'Madam,' he answers gravely, 'of this only God can be certain. What is your country?'

I ask him if there's a hospital nearby.

'Oh yes,' he affirms, 'a very fine hospital, one of the finest in India. It has all the modern equipments. Topnotch.'

'Can we carry him there?' I ask.

'Oh no,' he replies, taken aback. 'The hospital is very far. It is being back in Panjim.'

...

So that is how we found ourselves traveling back along the same road we'd come down in the morning, nursing someone else's injured child, in someone else's Dodge utility.

Before leaving Calangute, the policemen's discovery of Qasim's keys, still dangling from the ignition, had very nearly sealed a different fate for us. They saw it as confirmation of our ownership of the vehicle, and hence also of our culpability in the accident. We were charged with failure to produce certificates of ownership, with driving an unauthorized vehicle, and with failure to supplement our international driver's licenses with a Goanese driving permit. We sat glumly in Calangute's musty police station, filling out forms in triplicate, fully expecting to be consigned to a lifetime of oblivion in some choleric Goan prison, rats nibbling our ears.

But we had not counted on the doctor, and his belated sense of urgency about the boy. The tourists must drive him to Panjim now, he'd insisted, or this little boy will be dying. At first the police were unmoved. They were enjoying the drama of our arrests. But some money changed hands, some intense negotiating went on between the doctor and Rob and the local constabulary, some more money changed hands, and then we were free.

In Panjim, thanks to the doctor, we were able to circumvent the queue in casualty. Anxiously we awaited a verdict on the little boy. I feared he would be a cripple, perhaps brain-damaged; the six hours that had elapsed since the collision could well have compromised his recovery. Finally, the locum emerged to tell us that the child had regained consciousness.

We smiled at each other, overjoyed.

Whether the multiple fractures to his femur, tibia and fibula could be properly re-set, the locum continued, or whether the limb would require amputation due to excessive blood loss, it was too soon to say.

I burst into tears.

'Do not cry, Madame,' said the locum. 'Your tourniquet may well have saved him,' he said, pointing to my skirt.

What if he doesn't survive? I asked Rob tearfully on the way back to Anjuna. He didn't seem to have any relatives.

We had taken Qasim's ute. Rob was driving.

He sought to reassure me. 'He'll live, he said. Believe me.'

'What if he loses his leg?'

'No big deal,' said Rob. 'He can always make a living as a beggar.'

When we reach Anjuna I expect we shall stay in the little beachfront hostel Rob remembers from his last visit. The air will be wailing with guitars from the Music House and masked partygoers will float past us like dark wraiths. But we will barely have enough energy left to undress, to fold our bodies down upon the mats and lie with the Arabian Sea pounding in our ears. By the time Anjuna Markets comes around again, one week from today, I'll already have left Mysore to catch my plane home.

CHAPTER 2

FROM BANGKOK TO BANGED UP

Matt Towner

Bangkok was crazy in those days. Not that it isn't crazy today, but it's a different sort of crazy now. I spent many years back and forth from Bangkok in the early 1990s; in the days before the internet and mobile phones took over the world. Jewelers in the wealthy western world needed gem-dealing gypsies like us to bring them opals, diamonds, sapphires, rubies and all the bells and whistles that came with them. We smuggled them in and out of war zones and corrupt countries. We negotiated with beggars and thieves through to cartels and characters on every side of the planet. The beauty of gem dealing is that so many colorful countries have stones that no other country has: Australia for opals, Thailand for sapphires, Burma for rubies, Colombia for emeralds, and the list goes on. Before the internet, jewelers in America, Europe, Australia, Japan needed dealers like us to bring them stones from far out places. Now they can Google them and have them delivered. It was a different world and we loved it.

I fell in to stone smuggling, literally. I was meandering down the Monasteraki Markets in Athens when a stallholder storyteller called me to his stand like a pied piper, and I a wide-eyed wanderer. I not only bought bags of his treasures but we wined and dined, enjoying everything Athens had to offer. By the time I sobered up, I was back and forth from Bangkok, bringing backpacks full of stones to the market stallholders and jewelers, not just in Athens and the Greek Islands, but all over Europe, then on to America and Australia, but always back and forth to Bangkok. We used to call it our office.

Khao San Road was like a village back then, within the hustle and bustle, beeping horns and drug busts of Bangkok. We knew everyone and everyone knew us. 'Carlos the Portuguese' as he was famously known, had been setting up office on the street for 20 years before I came along. I was the new kid on the rocks and loving every minute of it. We would fly in and out of the Thai international airport every week when we were really working it: India for stones and silver one week, then Bali the next week for more ornate jewelry. Nepal the week after that, where we had a jeweler whose uncle was the master craftsman making one-off pieces for the King, full-time for his whole life. His father had done so before him and his son was being trained to do so after him, as had been the tradition for generation after generation. So, our jeweler, 'The Nephew of Nepal' as we called him, worked in the same workshop, making special pieces for us alongside the creations for the King.

But the greatest find for Carlos and I was the 'Chinese Wheel of Life'. Again, wording that we created to showcase a selection of gemstone donuts we found in Hong Kong. Honkers, in those days,

From Bangkok to Banged Up

was the sales office for anything and everything made in China. The golden gates to China were well and truly closed to Westerners, especially to business, but Hong Kong was like a showroom of everything. For gemstones, Kowloon had whole office towers full of stones in every shape and size, from earring studs to life-size carvings of horse and cart, all made from solid stone. The gemstone donuts were exactly that. Every semiprecious stone you can think of from amethyst to rose quartz, lapis lazuli to obsidian, all in perfect circles with nice neat holes in the middle. The beauty of them was not just natural but practical. The hollow centerpieces meant that leather cord could be easily looped through to create quick and easy gemstone jewelry. And for the more up-market market, 'The Nephew of Nepal' handmade us gold and silver attachments and chains to match.

We would buy the gemstone donuts in bulk, 80 kilos each at a time, and negotiated a price at US50 cents per piece. We would carry 80 kilos each in our backpacks back to Bangkok, where we would sell them wholesale for US$10 apiece. We already had a steady market of reliable buyers. Not just the stallholders of the street markets all over that crazy city, but more so all the market traders from Japan and Europe and Australia, who would fly in for a weekend and buy everything from us as we had stones and silver, gold and goblets, from the best of Thai silver to Bali bracelets, Indian antique jewelry to Nepalese royalties. Our 'Chinese Wheel of Life' outsold everything, and everything is all about supply and demand. We were flying back and forth from Bangers to Honkers every week, then needed more and more stock so we offered a couple of great mates of ours to carry for us and with us.

Now, let me confirm that although we were smuggling, we were not really doing anything too illegal. We never carried drugs, and why would we, with mark-ups from US50 cents to US$10 dollars and selling out in days. We were avoiding tax to be sure, but really, who doesn't if you can? Plus, it was a different world back then. Airports were much more free and easy. In fact, I remember flying from Bangkok to Amsterdam, which we did every year for the Queen's Birthday. On that one weekend the whole of Amsterdam city becomes a giant festival complete with market stalls on every street and square. Traders like us would fly in in advance from all over the world, arriving days before to reserve a great space, ready for our red velvet carpets covered in colorful stones. As always, Carlos and I had 80 kilos of stones in each of our backpacks. Customs was easy but the hard part was looking like a backpacker whilst carrying 80 kilos from baggage carousel to taxi rank. My years of rugby came in handy for the clean and jerk. Subtle deep breath, then hoist the heavy backpack up on to one shoulder and onto my back, then walk. This one particular trip, some commotion happened at customs and I arrived at the taxi rank still with my passport in my hand. No-one had checked me at all. Not my bags, not my documents, not even a word. Can you imagine that today? A different world indeed.

Bangkok was often almost just as easy. With the 'wheel of life' business rolling on so quickly and strongly, the four of us had flown to Hong Kong. Carlos and I, and to be totally honest I cannot remember the fourth flyer, and the hero of the story I have not seen since, so as with all of my stories, the names are always changed to protect the guilty. Unless the hero has read my story and is happy to be named, as with our superhero, 'Carlos the Portuguese'. So, let's call our third wheel Alberto, and our fourth wheel will not matter for this story, as you shall see. On these trips we always traveled separately so as not to look like a gang; or would we be a garnet? What is the word for a group of gem dealers? Either way, we would clean and jerk alone and head to customs separately, as strangers.

If anyone remembers Bangkok International Airport in the early 1990s, it was a giant mezzanine with customs at the bottom of escalators from the flight arrival areas above. I was already at customs, passport in hand, when I heard a crazy crash. As I turned to the heavens above, I saw Alberto at the top of the escalators in a state of shock, and a wonderful waterfall of gemstone donuts cascading down the stairs in every color of the rainbow. His backpack had burst and 80 kilos of stones fell through the bottom of his bag down the escalators, into the arms of awaiting customs.

Then there were three. We kept our calm and crept through customs and out to the taxi rank and back to Khao San Road, all the while worried about poor Alberto. Thailand then, and still now, is a very strict country in many ways, and very loose in others. Like most of the countries we bought stones from, corruption was the key. In fact, Carlos and I had specially made leather belts, like cowboys would wear but with zips on the inside where we would fold and carry US$20,000 just in case we ever needed it. Luckily, we never did, but Alberto had no such belt and no such money, and that we knew for sure. We also knew that, like us, he was smuggling nothing but stones. So hopefully jail would not be on the cards but any trouble in a Third World country is like playing poker. In Alberto's case strip poker, for sure!

As we forecast his fate, wondering whether we would ever see him again – remember, these were the days before the robots took over, so no internet or emails, mobile phones or off-my-Facebook – there was no way to contact someone other than make a meeting place somewhere in the world and be there. Queen's Day in Amsterdam was that for many of us, but that was once a year. Our office in Bangkok, as we jokingly but lovingly called it, was a streetside table at a bar and restaurant. We would sit there day and night dealing gemstones to the myriad of merchants who came through town, either in and out just to stock up and run back to their hot spot street stalls or jewelry shops all over the world, or often on to Ko Pha Ngan for a full moon party before going back to the real world. Sometimes our table would swell to hold a dozen daring day and night traders, and go from business to pleasure. Full seafood banquets and bottles of vodka with buckets of ice, and a sweet little mixer that was basically legal speed!

It was called Lipovitan and it really got the party started and kept it going all night long. The little bottle with a big kick had a foretelling symbol of a red bull. Yes, you guessed it; the European entrepreneur who was there at the time spent years jumping through hoops to export the energy drink, but rumors of formaldehyde inside, which was used to embalm mummies way back when, meant that he had to refine the recipe somewhat, but boy did he make a lot. On these dinner party nights that were pretty much every night, as a treat for dessert, Carlos would call on one of the street beggars selling red roses. When I say call, these humble street sellers were often deaf and most times disabled in some way. So, to see their faces light up with joy every time Carlos would buy the whole bucket of roses for the table was a treat better than ice-cream.

But this night was not one of those nights. It was somber; as was the state of Alberto. Not as sad and sorry as the night one of our South American brothers fell asleep at the table, or so we thought, as we continued the party all around him, not worrying to disturb him as he could sleep through anything. It was only when the bill came and we were all ready for the next bar, infamously called 'Hello Bar', we realized that we actually had to say…goodbye. Heroin killed many on that road, if you took that path. Pretty much every day there was a dead body in a bed, but not usually at the bar. Thailand attracts a lot of different people for a lot of different reasons and heroin is one of them. Not the worst of them unfortunately.

As per my introduction to this book and this series, I am not a big fan of swearing. My father says that if you use those words you are just lazy with vocabulary. My mother never swears at all. But I did take both my perfect parents on a gem dealing gypsy tour with me once; as I sold stones to jewelers they took in the sights. One of our stops was the Emerald Isle – Ireland not Colombia. After a great night of drinking and singing and laughing and loving life as the Irish do all so well, whilst all the while swearing like fuck drivers, pardon the pun, my sweet little mother said that it sounds okay when they F'ing C this and F'ing C that, as their accents put potty mouth to poetry.

But sometimes a description deserves a good swear word, as nothing else will do – like 'Crazy Sh*t', which we use lightheartedly as the title of this book series. But this is really crazy and deserves harsher words, because when I was based in Bangkok in the early

33

1990s, out every night meeting mad men and women and doing deals all day every day, there were stories that one could buy a 12-year-old girl and fuck her and kill her for $200. I say this not to shock you but to paint a harsh picture of what really was the Wild West of South-East Asia. The harsh reality is that in the farming regions only sons were seen as valuable to work the land. Daughters were often sold to the Bangkok brothels, or worse. We kept away from that scene as Khao San Road was the total opposite of Patpong – that was a pleasure center for perverts and priests (just kidding, but had to throw that one in). But seriously, it was often diplomats who were a haven for kiddy fiddlers disguised as foreign affairs. Foreign affairs all right.

We may not have had those types or the red lights on Khao San but we had the other type. Not just backpackers and market traders, wheelers and dealers from all over the world, but if you were a heroin addict and could get off the couch and save any cash then Bangkok was on the wish list. The problem is that the smack in Thailand is so much better, stronger, harder, faster; well, fast acting then slow moving. No matter how controlled and calculated a junkie you may be, if you take the same amount you would at home that is often the last purple haze before you turn blue.

The most traumatic overdose I remember was an Israeli guy we knew well who not only had a habit but also took that next fatal step. Funding any habit is hard, whether that is sailing or golfing, and each to their own. But once you start swallowing condoms full of gear and getting on planes to fund your habit, it's just not cricket. Again, it was a lot easier then, and in those days, I was often in hotel rooms in India, Nepal, Bangkok, Bali with people swallowing condoms of hash more than heroin. Life is all about risk and return for me, and the returns I was making gem smuggling, for a slap on the wrist if it all went wrong, outweighed any returns for risk of rectal exams in the Bangkok Hilton. But this Israeli daredevil got worse than that, as his condoms burst, which is bad in the heat of passion but worse hot with heroin. I still to this day can hear his girlfriend's screams as she woke the whole street, running up and down the road wailing like a siren. But it was way too late for an ambulance. It took us half a dozen laps of running up and down with her, Carlos on one side and me on the other, till she slowed down and quietened down enough for us to console her. They were dark days.

Anyway, back to the office. It was one of those nights. No bouquets of flowers or seafood banquet. A bucket of ice and vodka, red bull of course, with chasers of concern about the state of Alberto. As we sat in shock, shot after shot, not knowing where he was or how he was, all of a sudden like a stripper from a cake, out jumps Alberto from a runaway cab. We never took tuktuks, those things will kill you. It was a drive-by shooting of delight, especially seeing his big smiling face and outrageous accent fired from a Thai taxi. He was the Antonio Banderas of our band of gypsies and he always made me laugh. He spoke in broken English and had a passion for life, which saw him never afraid to ask questions. Many years later I learnt a great quote, that the quality of your life is determined by the quality of your questions; very true. I remember one wild night in a busy bar in Zurich, our secret spot in Switzerland where we would make 1000 Swiss francs in an hour selling stones on the street. Alberto was a ladies' man; well, weren't we all really? His rugged looks, husky voice and hot chocolate accent saw women swoon. But his broken English, and comprehension still with training wheels, always made for fun-filled conversations and confusions. He made up for any miss-hits by simply hitting on every woman in every bar. South American men are great at that. I was more of a quiet achiever; that dark, mysterious stranger in the corner, who looked like a cross between a cowboy and an Indian, with long hair and leather vest, cowboy boots and covered in gemstone jewelry.

Alberto came to my corner with a quizzical look on his face. This was nothing new so I was smiling already, amused in anticipation. In his wonderful way with words he asked, 'What is lesbian?' I was taken aback. I expected a laugh but not gay abandon. I fumbled to explain, not sure of his motives. 'A lesbian is a woman who loves women,' I replied, the quizzical look now on my face. His face lit up and he threw his hand in the air, as if in celebration, turned to the group of gorgeous girls he had been entertaining and at the top of his lustful Latin lungs he shouted in true Alberto style, 'I am lesbian! I love womans!'

He was enjoying his freedom as he exited the cab on Khao San and entered the office, our table on the street covered in glasses and gloom. Hugs and cheers, back patting and drinks orders all happened at once, like fireworks. When the smoke settled and the bang bang stopped, we had to hear the story. Once again Alberto's beautiful broken and bandaged English saved the day. Not wooing wonderful women this time, but tying up Thai customs in a way that only a few good men can. They could not handle the truth. He baffled them and bamboozled them in South American style, like a double-jointed salsa dancer at Mardi Gras. By the time he finished with them they did not know if they were coming or going or where he had come from and more importantly where to send him to.

They did keep all of his stones, well the gems that Carlos and I had paid for him to carry. That 80-kilo waterfall of wonder was now customs' Christmas presents for all airport staff, or more likely out the back door into the big boss's car, along with everything else they confiscated that day. They took all of his money, in fact his whole wallet and his watch and anything of any value. But in true Thai style, they gave him enough money for the taxi fare to the office and here we were. The three musketeers and the guy I can't remember...must be D'Artagnan?

So, Alberto was screwed. And not the way he liked to be. Another positive though was that they may have taken all of his possessions but did not take his pride. His juggling act of accent and emotion saved him from the rubber glove of love, which could have been performed passionately by an over-amorous customs official searching unofficially. But he was broke and literally was left with the clothes on his back. We were all used to well-worn wardrobes. When you carry 80 kilos of stones there is no room for a clotheshorse, not even a Shetland. Carlos had a trick that he would top his pack with dirty undies. So, if customs did ever open his bag that first sight for sore eyes would put anyone off digging deeper.

In the near ten years that I smuggled stones all over the world I was only ever opened a handful of times. Every time I talked my way through and never lost a stone, not even a kidney stone. Sorry that's a bad dad joke. If we flew into Athens, which we often did, we would look as much like drug smugglers as we possibly could.

Athens International Airport had two sets of customs, one just for drugs and another just for duties. Our aim was to get pulled for drugs. We would then stand back and wait and watch as those drugs guys would dig through a whole bag full of gemstones without a second glance or a third degree. By the time they had finished going through everything with a fine toothcomb and a pitchfork, the duties desk was packed up and gone, and so were we.

I got opened coming back into Australia once. Bris Vegas, a nickname for Brisbane, as all Australians have, and an ironic one of course, as that big country town was nothing like Las Vegas. My gorgeous girlfriend and I convinced the kind customs people that we had collected the treasure chests we carried so as to create one giant mural as a wonder wall in our new home and they happily let us through. Now before any do-gooders get too outraged, it's not like we were smuggling the crown jewels. That comes later. We had backpacks full of semiprecious stones ,so maybe $10,000 tops. The duties and taxes we were avoiding would have been a few thousand dollars tops, and in fact on rough stone there was no duty. Sure, if we then sold those stones all retail, piece by piece, we could make $100,000. But most often we would wholesale the lot as quickly as possible and be back on a plane.

Later in my gem-dealing career I became an 'opalholic'. Not that I planned to but hey who does? It's just that every bar I walked into, as soon as anyone heard my accent they wanted opals. So, people get what people want if you want to satisfy supply and demand and make great money on the way. The beauty of moving from semiprecious to precious stones was that rather than carrying and clean and jerking 80 kilos of stones from carousels, I could carry

$100,000 worth of stones in a gun holster under my business shirt. I did get opened going in to Germany once and they did find my holster, much to their surprise. They certainly surprised me how quickly they drew their guns...German precision, like Swiss watches. The key to any good smuggle is to stay calm always. *'Meine Deutsche ist nicht sehr gut aber manchmal ich vehrstahn.'* In true Alberto style, my well-worn one liner in German, but with my strongest Australian accent, always gets a laugh, even under imminent gunfire. *'Ich arbiter mit Australicher opalen.'* Translated as crudely as spoken means 'My German is not very good but sometimes I understand. I work with Australian opals'. Just like Alberto, once people stop laughing, I go in for the close but usually mild-mannered jewelers in their fancy stores, or lovely ladies in beautiful bars – not usually storm trooper style customs officials with Glocks drawn, chiseled jaws and rock-hard stares. I reverted to English, as I always do after those opening lines. This time I explained that my over the shoulder boulder holder was exactly that. I was carrying opals not pistols and I came bearing gifts. Everywhere I go, everywhere I stay, the people I meet, and the places I love, I give the gift that keeps on giving, the rainbow serpent, and the spirit of Australia, and I happily gifted a few boulder opals to those border guards.

Carlos and I gifted every night. He was an incredible mentor for me, not just for gem dealing and traveling as capitalist hippies, as we did so well, and I still proudly am today. Carlos had a great quote: 'Money is my slave, I am not the slave of money.' So many nights all over the world we would make thousands of dollars in a few hours then find the funniest bar in town. High end, low end, middle ground, did not matter as long as it was fun, and then we made it more fun. Especially if we were new to a town, from A to Z, Athens to Zurich, Bangkok to Byron Bay, I cannot count the number of times I heard that sound. Oh no, here we go again. Carlos would jump up on the bar and with the body language of Robin Hood and the same intentions shout, 'Drinks for everyone!'

This night in Bangkok we would be shouting drinks too. Alberto has no money and forgotten man had forgotten his wallet. But Alberto had a plan. If we could lend him US$20,000 and pay his flights he could fly home to Colombia, buy emeralds, or ezmeralds as he called them in Albertonese, then fly straight to Switzerland and we would all make a small fortune. We would meet at Queen's Day in Amsterdam as we always did but party more than ever before. My father 'Rockin Rod', a born salesman himself, always says that sales people are the easiest people to sell to, as they love a good sales pitch. Alberto had us at Hello, well at the Hello Bar in Bangkok, and his pitch was perfect. We all shook hands over several more shots and Alberto flew to Colombia the very next day on borrowed money and borrowed time.

Now if you thought South-East Asia was a dodgy place to be wheeling and dealing, South America was a whole different ball game. Forget ball tampering, over there they'll steal your whole damn game. Gringos – we foreigners – get burned there as quickly as a Buddha stick in a bathhouse. But I knew Brazilian gem dealers who in their own country would have to change address, move apartments every month. As soon as too many people knew who they were and what they did it was time to go, as an armed hold-up was only arm's distance away.

Alberto landed in his hometown in Colombia and taxied straight to the Emerald Mine, which he knew well. As was his plan and his promise, he purchased US$20,000 worth of the best emeralds our money could buy. All was perfect, as was his pitch. In the taxi on his way back to the airport, on his way then to Switzerland to sell the fine gems to jewelers for a mighty fine profit, the wheels came off. Not literally, but badly. The Colombian cab driver simply pulled over to the side of the road, all four wheels well and truly intact, turned in his seat, pulled a gun and said, 'Give me the ezmeralds.' Alberto had been had. A set-up from the get-go. The mine had not only undermined him and double-crossed him but also overthrown everything.

Luckily for Alberto, similar to the situation in Bangkok, the taxi driver took everything but was kind enough to drop him back to the airport in time for his flight to Zurich. For the second time in as many days, Alberto was leaving an international airport with nothing, not a cent, not a stitch, not a clue. But he had another idea.

Of course, we knew nothing of this. We were still in Bangkok back and forth to Hong Kong, cashing in on donuts and stocking up for a Queen's Day fit for a king. Without jungle drums there was no international communication when you were on the road in those days. We never sat still long enough to receive postcards, although we sent them every now and again, just to let loved ones know that we were still alive. A reverse-charge call from a public phone was possible every now and then, but again, we had no phones to receive them and could only make them if anyone would take them. If only Alberto had called. Why didn't you call?

Alberto forgot to phone a friend but pitched another great idea. Flat broke in the richest country in the world, now there's an oxymoron, with all due respect. Admittedly it's never hard to find money in Switzerland. Hell, I've had ten-year-old kids come up and buy hundreds of dollars' worth of jewelry from a street stall like they're buying lollipops. One such day, Carlos and I had made several thousand dollars selling stones on the street, the beautiful cobblestoned streets of the Niederdorf. As Carlos loved to do, we proceeded to the finest restaurant we could find just to watch the doorman's doubt and the patrons' pretense as we ordered the best of everything on the menu. As I waited and watched, entertaining and enjoying the gorgeous girls we had at our table, Carlos came running back from the bathroom flapping like an Olympic flag in a winning way. 'Let's go…let's go…let's go,' he said. Our fast departure left the whole restaurant as baffled as our timely arrival.

It was only when we got out on to the streets, those spotless streets, that Carlos explained that as he sat to think, he did think that he would love a cigarette as he went through the motions. Like magic, there on the toilet-roll holder was a packet of cigarettes. But as he opened the packet, which had just popped up, out popped not nicotine but cocaine. And a lot of it. It was the first time that I had ever had cocaine and we danced all night from salsa to sunrise. I will never forget the next day as Carlos threw what was left out the window of our moving car, a kombi we called Hotel California. In a father–son style talk, as he was and still is 20 years my senior and my mentor, he told me that he had learnt that coca can cause chaos in more ways than one.

This was Alberto's Plan C. After the wheel of life waterfall then the ezmerald debacle had both left him penniless, he borrowed Swiss francs from another kind crew and flew back to Bogota again. This time to as much as possible of their other expensive export. Not emeralds, not coffee, but cocaine. Third time unlucky for Alberto. But saying that, things could have been worse. I am sure that Swiss jails are much more comfortable than Colombian cells. In any case, Alberto should well and truly be out by now and I hope that his luck has changed. That crazy king never arrived for our Queen's Day. We only heard the stories. Like Facebook posts, but face to face. That's the only way we learnt things then and some of us learnt the hard way.

CHAPTER 3

WELCOME TO CAMBODIA

Feather Kibby

I had always had an interest in exploring South-East Asia, but somehow my love for Thailand had never seen me cross the borders beyond my mango sticky rice. I had found myself in Thailand six times, with a vague idea of all the hidden treasures beyond it: Laos, Cambodia, Vietnam. I had many friends who had visited Cambodia, from those who went traveling on their 'gap' year circuit, celebrating their newfound freedom, to those who deeply immersed themselves in the culture for months, volunteering at orphanages; I had heard only positive reviews. Being the traveler that I am, I knew one day I would get there.

Two years ago I was back home in Australia, with an invitation to my cousin's wedding in Thailand. Of course, it was with pure delight that I accepted, and began to think of all the places I could explore that I had yet to. I looked at the dates and realized that an opportunity had arisen that could mean I finally crossed that border.

How I choose to travel, is through recommendations from friends. The one and only time I took a *Lonely Planet* with me was on my first trip to South America, back when I was 18. Since then, I haven't traveled by the guides but on the advice of my friends, or of those I've met on the road. So I knew it was finally time to ask all my friends where they would recommend visiting in Cambodia.

Months later, after saying goodbye to the love of my life (that wasn't meant to be) and leaving my family behind in a luxurious resort, I boarded a plane, with farewells to the comfort of Thailand, and to the people that knew me. Like every plane that I have boarded it comes with a mix of excitement and anxiety. When you travel, you are a blank canvas, a nobody in a sea of everybody, emotions heightened for the unknown. I really had no idea what to expect and nor did I want to know; expectations had ruined a few too many experiences in my life and with every disappointment I had made promises to myself not to have expectations. I boarded the plane with an open heart and open mind, eager for what lay ahead, eager to finally leave the comfort and the familiarity of Thailand and venture beyond.

I landed in Phnom Penh in the afternoon, after too many stopovers on a cheap flight (direct flights being one of the many conveniences one must sacrifice in order to lead a true gypsy life). Straight away the chaos of a capital city of Asia hit me, in only the way a capital city in Asia can. There was an immediate feeling of desperation towards travelers because somehow the color of your skin has defined you as a walking dollar sign. However, there was an underlying sadness to this desperation that I hadn't noticed before, an emptiness that comes with the horrible history of the Khmer Rouge that is present in Cambodia.

I didn't want to pass judgment too quickly; that is, until I realized all the cab drivers were asking me about triple the price of what I needed to pay to get to where I had to go. (When I went to Vietnam the year before, I got into a cab as soon as I arrived, was dropped at my hotel, paid the driver $60 and then was told at reception the route should have cost me $12!)

I had learnt my lesson, to always inquire how much it will cost you to travel to your accommodation from your first point of arrival. It takes a lot of practice and patience when traveling to not get overly frustrated when EVERYBODY is trying to rip you off, but it's something that over time you can come to peace with by having an understanding they are only trying to look after themselves.

I refused to spend what they were asking, so I walked about 20 minutes out of the airport, found myself on a highway, and then jumped into an open-ended truck with a bunch of other Westerners, that just happened to pull over on the side of the highway.

I was staying in a place downtown that had been recommended by a friend, a hostel, but with private rooms (in my later years of travel I had given up shared hostel rooms). I checked in and was taken to my room which was basic Asian style – super small, dingy, a window that could slightly open, with stagnant air from the streets below seeping in. The bathroom, as anyone who has been to Asia knows, was the typical, cringeworthy style of showering over the toilet, ensuring that no matter what, everything in the bathroom is ALWAYS wet. It was a defiant contrast to the fresh white sheets I had slept in at the hotel the night before!

I lay down on the bed and took a few moments, closing my eyes. I was exhausted. It had been a long day of traveling and I wanted nothing more than to keep my eyes shut and give way to sleep, however the adventurous spirit inside me refused to let this happen. Here I was in a brand new country, a brand new city, one that I had never explored, and I knew I couldn't ignore my desire to go out and see it for the first time.

It was around 4 pm by this time, and I also realized how hungry I was, having hardly eaten anything in my commute throughout the day. I had a quick shower and decided to head out for a casual walk in the neighborhood to get some food. I thought to myself, I would just take an hour outside and then get an early night, unaware the turn of events I was soon to find myself in.

I walked the streets for around half an hour, getting a feel for the neighborhood I was staying in, passing beggars on the street and small children wandering around, without a parent to be seen. It always surprises me in developing countries to see children in the streets and out until so late at night, without any parents in sight. I was scouting out a cafe to have an afternoon snack at, but decided to make a quick stop at a corner store as I was really thirsty from walking, and had no water.

I was looking in the fridges, trying to decide what drink to get; I always love trying new and foreign or strange-looking foods and drinks when I am way, anything to get me out of my comfort zone. While I was deciding between a lychee juice and another strange looking purple fruit drink, a lady approached me. She looked to be Cambodian and asked me where I was from. I smiled politely and told her I was from Australia.

'Australia!' she exclaimed.

'I have heard so many good things about Australia, do you mind if I talk to you?'

'Of course not,' I answered.

We sat together on the small bench, looking out to the street in front of us. She asked me questions about Australia, and I was only too happy to share with her a little about my life. She told me that her sister was about to move to Australia to study nursing. She then went on to ask me if I would like to go to her house to meet her sister because she would be so interested to ask me questions about the new land she was about to move to.

I felt fatigue setting in, a heaviness in my eyes and there was a part of me that really wanted to say no. Then she asked me if I was hungry, and I could feel the emptiness of my stomach. Well I thought, the idea of going to a local's house for dinner, with a local family, for my first night in Cambodia sounded like an adventure I couldn't refuse.

I smiled at this sweet new friend of mine, so small in contrast to me, petite and kind. She was generous enough to pay for my drink (I had decided on the lychee) so without any further hesitation I agreed to go with her. She was very excited by my decision and quickly ushered me outside.

Before I knew it, I was on the back of a motorbike with a total stranger, in a completely foreign country, just hours after my arrival. Well I really believe in the good of people, so there was no doubt in my mind that I was doing the right thing. I did think to myself that I must pay attention to the route we were going, so I could attempt to find my way home. Those of you who have been to any Asian city would know this is by no means easy, and after a few too many intersections and the chaos of way too many bikers on the road, I stopped trying to figure it out, and just assumed that if she was driving me far from where I was staying that she would be kind enough to drive me back.

The motorbike ride was about 20 minutes, and we made small chitchat the whole time, mainly her asking me questions all about my life. We arrived at a house that was typical of an Asian house. Brick, tall, somewhat unfinished, sparsely furnished and oddly decorated. An outdoor staircase led me into a simple, large room upstairs. At the door, when I went inside, was a sweet five-year-old girl. The woman led me into the main room and I was introduced to her brother. She then left, and I was left alone in the room with this man.

He smiled at me warmly and said, 'Please, come sit down,' so I sat on the only couch. We made polite conversation for some time about my life, Australia, what I was doing in Cambodia.

Presently his sister brought in a simple dish of rice and veggies and said to us, 'Here is your dinner, come sit.'

The man and I moved to small table in the same room. The woman and the man then exchanged some small words, and she disappeared. This was the last I saw of her, nor did I ever see the child again.

Over our dinner the conversation diverted to what he did for a living. He began to talk in a language that I was not familiar with in the slightest, and that was the world and lingo of gambling. He explained that he had worked for the casinos for many years, traveling all over the world doing so, and people like James Packer (and others) had played at his table.

I could tell I was meant to be impressed by his gambling knowledge and experiences, but I could feel the heaviness of my eyes, and the fatigue of traveling was starting to make my mind drift. I thought back to my simple hostel room and how I longed to just take a shower over the toilet, and lie down.

However, I had put myself in this situation, and like many ridiculous situations I somehow find myself in, I knew I had to see it through. I questioned him about the 'sister' and the little girl, but he dismissed me. I was slightly confused as to where the other sister was, the one I was meant to be meeting, the one that wanted to know everything about Australia.

I kept nodding politely, smiling when needed, as he rambled on about his gambling career, thrusting his business card in my face, to prove his work.

After some time he asked me if I wanted to learn to play. I thought it would be too rude to decline his offer, and so moments later I found myself sitting opposite him while he taught me a simple game to do with cards and money. (Not having the slightest interest in gambling, I am unable to recall the name of the game.) He then went on to explain that the previous night he had been the card dealer at the nearby casino for a very rich lady from Singapore, and she was coming over soon, to play another game, with some other gamblers. It was her last night in Cambodia and she wanted to play a game. (Alarm bells really should have rung by now; I mean, looking back on it, I was really silly to believe that such a lady would come all the way to a card dealer's house just to gamble.)

Presently, his phone rang, and when he began to talk, a look of utter annoyance came over his face. Words were hastily spoken, and then he hung up.

He turned to me, 'Well that was the other gamblers, they are unable to make it, and this woman from Singapore is going to be here soon, would you be happy to play her?'

He continued, 'What we can do is I can play the cards right and offer you certain signs and whatever you win we can split. We are likely to be able to win around 10,000 dollars, that would be 5000 each.'

Okay, so just to recap, for those readers who may be a bit lost. The gamblers are a no-show, this local Cambodian man, whose house I have somehow found myself at, wants me to gamble in a game with some rich lady from Singapore, and assuming that he gives me certain symbols I am likely to win $10,000!

It seemed too bizarre and too surreal.

He went on, '$10,000 to this lady is nothing, she owns many hotels in Singapore, to her, losing that amount of money will not make a difference in her life, but to us, imagine how much that could help us.'

I began to see his reasoning. Okay, so he wanted me to cheat; was I a cheater? With his little signs, could I really win $10,000? This was all unraveling so fast that I didn't have the chance to logically think it through, then suddenly the doorbell rang.

'Quickly,' he said, 'come through here.'

And I followed him to another small room where there was a table in the middle, a bed to one side, and a bench to the other. He left the room and returned moments later with a small women, who was covered in make-up and wearing pearls. He introduced me to her and explained to her the situation and how the other gamblers hadn't turned up but I would be happy to play her. She looked surprised and looked me up and down.

'Well then, I suppose you will have to do, but do you have money to play with? Whatever you put down I will match.'

I smiled politely and took a $50 American note out of my bag, the only money I had.

'Is this all you have?' she asked.

'Well,' interjected my new gambling team member, 'you see, she has lots more money, but it's at her hotel. I am sure she can go get it in due course, I will lend her $200 and the rest we will just keep tabs.'

'Yes, I do, it's true, I have much more money at my hostel, it's just in my bank, so I need to go get my ATM card that's all,' I hurriedly gushed, now somewhat nervous, yet excited to continue the game.

We began the game, and I put my $50 into the middle, and the woman matched it. We played our first round, and of course I won, so she wanted to put more money in. I used the $200 I had borrowed, and the woman kept matching it. At this stage we were taking tabs and writing all the money that I owed, as if it was actually present.

The rounds went on, and they went fast. While we were playing she was chatting to me about all the hotels she owned in Singapore and how I must come stay. I thought to myself how great it was to now have a contact in Singapore!

We continued to play, moving so fast I barely had time to think about my cards before the round was over. I was going with the flow, following my new friend's lead, while this woman kept dishing out $100 bills and raising the stakes higher. Of course I kept winning, and suddenly it would seem I was thousands of dollars up, and was about to somehow make $5000 if I won the next round.

My heart was beating so loudly by this stage, I swear everyone in the room could have heard it, everything had happened so fast that I couldn't really comprehend what was going on.

We were about to play the last round, which would somehow mean me winning everything and her losing all the money she had put down. At this stage I had only 'IOU' notes.

'Stop,' she suddenly said. 'I want to see the money before we continue to play. You do actually have it don't you?'

'Yes I assured her, it just requires me to go home.'

'Okay, well why don't you do that and we can meet back here in an hour.'

By now I had around $2000 that I was supposedly meant to have put down.

I turned to my friend.

'Yes,' he agreed. 'That's a good idea, why don't you go and I will get someone to take her back to her hostel on a motorbike, so she can collect money and then meet back here.'

'Perfect,' she responded.

'Meet me back here in an hour, with all your money and we will finish the game.'

She scooped up her handbag and walked out the door.

As soon as she left I took a moment to take in a deep breath and try and comprehend what had just unfolded. It was only that morning I was in basking in a swimming pool with my family.

'Are you sure this is going to work?' I asked. 'I mean, it seems a bit risky for me to hand over all my money. What if we lose?'

'No, not possible,' was his response. 'You have already won so much, it is just the last round and I can assure you, you will win.' 'All it takes is you going to the ATM and withdrawing $2000 and then we will play, and then we are going to win $10,000 back! It completely flawless.'

He had a big smile on his face and seemed so excited by the prospects of our win and what it could bring to him and his family.

'Okay,' I said, 'I believe you, I just need someone to take me home.' 'Yes I will call someone, and you can collect what you need and then go to an ATM on the way back, we also need you to bring your passport.'

That was a strange request I thought to myself, but one that I bypassed. I could hear the heartbeat in my ears, my palms were sweaty but I was also convinced I was about to walk away $10,000 richer.

He made a quick call and soon enough I was on the back of a motorbike, with two new ladies who I had not met before, zooming into the nighttime traffic of the bustling city. As I turned around to look back at the house, I saw him standing on the balcony, and there was something in his look, something slightly menacing, that for the first time made me question my moves.

On the bike back, I again made small chat with the ladies; they decided to drop me at the top of my street where I was staying, with clear instructions to get my passport and my bankcards. They would meet me again in 15 minutes and take me back to the house via the ATM.

I rushed up the stairs and back into my room. I sat on the bed for a moment trying to think straight about what to do. Everything had happened so fast, and I was so tired I couldn't think straight. I really wanted to ask somebody for advice, but as I had just arrived I had had no chance to make any friends. I opened my laptop with the hope of trying to reach out to someone back home, but the time difference ensured there was no-one online to chat to.

I thought to myself I would just take the card, take out some money, but not all of it, and not take my passport. Leaving my passport behind made me feel a bit more reassured.

I met back up with the ladies and hopped on to the back of their bike. As we drove off I glanced behind me at a lady selling food on the side of the road. Without them seeing her, she shook her head very directly. Could I have been imagining it? Was that headshake for me?

I started to get nervous. Here I was on the back of a bike, with strangers I had never met, in a foreign country, with nobody knowing where I was, about to take out all my money.

Okay, logic set in for the first time.

This didn't seem real. This couldn't really be happening. This is far from normal. I thought back to when I had seen the man standing on the balcony and the look on his face, and thought of the woman in the street shaking her head at me.

They stopped at an ATM and suddenly I hesitated.

'What is wrong?' they asked. 'Take out the $2000 as you have been instructed.'

Suddenly I felt sick and nervous, I felt uncomfortable but I didn't know how I was going to get out of this situation. I told them in a weak voice that I hadn't noticed the time and actually I was meeting friends now. They looked confused, frustrated, and then angry.

'No, no, no you are meant to get the money and come home with us right now. Let us call the boss.'

Suddenly I was on the phone to the man, with him asking me why I was hesitating. I managed to stammer my reply of meeting friends.

'Do you know what you are about to lose? Do you know what this can mean for us? For you? Or my family? Think what you can do with $10,000. For me, I can send my daughter to school and support my family, you are helping us all out so much, please do this for me, the money is nothing to this woman.'

Now I was really confused. I started to feel pity and guilt; was I really ruining this man's future? But then my logic stepped in again; no, this man was blackmailing me. He was trying to make me feel guilty; he was trying to steal my money.

'Look,' I began in a stern voice, 'I need to go meet my friends for dinner or they will be worried about me. I will make a spot to meet you in two hours.'

'Okay,' he replied. 'Arrange with the ladies and they will come collect you. I will call the woman and make sure she is okay with this.'

I passed the phone back to them and they said something quickly then hung up. I backed away from the ATM and boldly said with all the confidence I could muster, 'I will meet you back where you dropped me in two hours.'

'Yes, we will see you then, the exact spot, and don't forget to get the money.'

I nodded and turned my back, slowly walking away.

As soon as I turned the corner I began to run, without any idea where I was headed for, where I was in the city, I knew I just had to get away. I couldn't believe how stupid I had been to fall for such a prank, I couldn't believe how much faith I had put into these people. I couldn't believe I had almost fallen for it.

I was scared, nervous, anxious and suddenly very lonely. I was walking quickly and absent-mindedly, when I came across another tourist. I went up to him and asked if he spoke English and if I could talk to him for a moment. I then, very hurriedly, rattled off my whole story about what had happened. I was in tears and shaking, shocked from the whole experience.

He very calmly explained to me that it's a known thing to happen. It's the Malaysians who do it and they are con artists who literally prey on unsuspecting tourists (such as myself) and take all their money. I was lucky to get out of it without actually handing any of my money over. He suggested I take a taxi back to where I was staying and let the reception know what happened and stay there for the night.

I went home and, embarrassed, told the reception the situation I had landed myself in. I was slightly nervous, as the women knew where I was staying and I was worried they would come back to find me, but the hostel staff were so lovely they assured me I would be safe.

Somebody else staying at the hostel got wind of my story and wanted to know all about it, who they were, what they looked like. He had been attempting to find out who these people were because apparently it was a big problem and many tourists had been affected. Together we looked it up on the internet and sure enough there were many stories about situations almost mirroring mine.

After a few hours of talking about it, I was so exhausted and drained by the situation, I had to get to bed. I booked an early bus out of there, wanting to leave the city far behind me.

I retired to my room; my head hung low, my spirits crushed. Here was I thinking that I had made friends with locals within hours of arriving in a new country, but rather I had come moments from handing over my whole life savings! Was it my karma for agreeing to scam the whole gambling game? I could have stood my ground and said it was unjust and wrong and stepped away from the whole situation, so perhaps I deserved it.

I had a shower and lay down in bed decompressing the whole situation. It had all unraveled so quickly.

I felt like an idiot. I was an idiot, a total, stupid idiot tourist. I hated being a tourist. Usually I would couch surf and stay with locals, spending lengths of time in places and be more involved in their culture. Not for this trip. This trip I was a tourist, merely passing through on my way back home from the wedding; surely an act of idiocy could only happen to tourists. Many a time I have had friends ask me if I have ever been in really sketchy situations. No, I would always answer proudly. I was the kind of person who would leave all their bags with a stranger to go to the bathroom, the type of traveler who would opt to stick out their thumb and hitch a ride, rather than take the bus. The type of traveler who stayed with locals they had never met, and someone who, no matter what, somehow managed to always end up in ridiculous situations. However usually the ridiculous situations weren't dangerous ones.

I had a firm belief that if you believe in the kindness of strangers, if you have no fear that something bad will happen, then nothing will. Positive thoughts send out positive vibrations, which create positive situations (if that doesn't sound too 'hippie').

Well I guess I could no longer proudly announce that I had never been in a sketchy situation.

I really had the lady selling food to thank. It was her headshake, seemingly directed towards me, that made me begin to question everything. I sent her a wish and thanks, hoping it would find her somehow. As I drifted off to sleep, I thought of mango and sticky rice, a delectable treat, found just over the border; the border that I had never crossed until that day.

Sometimes, perhaps it's just better to stick with what you know; and mango sticky rice is a pretty alright thing to be stuck with.

CHAPTER 4

CONFESSIONS OF A MASSAGE JUNKIE

Bronwyn Clifton

Thailand was my first introduction to massage. It was 1991 and I'd left my best friend in London, stopping off in Bangkok, then traveling around the islands, alone. I distinctly remember listening for English speaking voices when I was on the plane, but there was no joy. The plane seemed to be packed with businessmen speaking Korean or Japanese, wearing suits. As we landed I was shitting myself.

Walking through the airport I was sweating and terrified. Even though Jennifer and I had successfully found our way, or should I say drunk our way, around a large portion of Europe and the United Kingdom, Asia was a whole new ball game. On the first stopover at Bangkok on the way to Amsterdam there'd been security guards with guns. Guns! It goes without saying this was light years before I had a mobile phone, prior to September 11 putting the fear of God into anyone boarding a plane.

'Hey, are you an Aussie?'

I heard a voice next to me speak, and I nearly jumped for joy. There stood a fair-haired young man, with a mullet, wearing thongs, a singlet and carrying a backpack. I could have hugged him. I've forgotten his name but for the sake of this story let's just call my knight in shining armor, Stuart. Within minutes of meeting, Stuart and I negotiated catching a cab to a hostel and then spent some time negotiating the madness of Bangkok together.

The capital of Thailand was typical of what people going to Asia expect: it was crowded, smelly, exotic and complicated. I loved it immediately. I had wanted to go to India and around Asia on my first big trip, but the friend I went with was obsessed with The Cure and yearned for the vibe of London, the greenery of Ireland and the timeless history of places like Italy, Germany and Greece. She won.

Not to be deterred, I planned a final stopover before returning home to a teaching job in the country and the reality of finding a new place to live, paying my bills and living a mundane life.

Bangkok was difficult to navigate after being in Europe, with signs on buses all written in Thai. Unlike Europe, Thai people weren't always able to converse in English. However, the tuktuks were a highlight. A bit like three-wheeled open-air taxis, we went in tuktuks all over the place at night, dodging and weaving amongst the crazy traffic. There were signs up warning Westerners not to hand over their passports as tuktuk drivers were infamous for taking them to jewelry stores and forcing unsuspecting travelers to buy jewelry. We survived – it was a terrific rush being in the warm open air, seeing the lights and shouting over the noise, bartering heavily with the drivers.

Even though my visit to Thailand was over 25 years ago a few things stand out. The bus ride to the ferry terminal was not for the faint hearted. I thought I would die many times over. At a run-down family-run cafe, an elderly Thai lady spilled a cup of tea on me. When I started to make a fuss, she laughed. It wasn't a mean laugh, she was telling me to get over myself. I liked it. The water was only tepid at any rate.

On the beach at Ko Samui I had a massage. I lay on the beach on warm sand, listening to the ocean, experiencing my first massage ever. It was administered by a middle-aged Thai woman. I'd found my nirvana. Her fingers worked my muscles, getting the knots out of my back and shoulders, and even caressed my feet. She used oil and crept up and down my spine, which resulted in a delightful feeling of blood rushing into my brain.

I'd been comfortable in hostel beds but no doubt my body had experienced a large amount of wear and tear, walking with a pack and traveling on buses, sleeping on ferries and planes. As I'd been walking around for the past six months I dread to think of how calloused my feet were but the woman did not seem to care; the people in Asian countries were so poor this was possibly her only source of income.

'You come back tomorrow, I braid your hair.'

I'd always been very tactile, and my hair was, and still is, very thick, long and wavy. The next day I returned and she deftly plaited my hair into hundreds of tiny little braids with beads. It took an hour and a half, but was an absolute blessing in the heat.

'You come back tomorrow, I have sarong.' And so it went on. I still have my faded sarong.

My mum has since reminded me that I was always a touchy-feely kind of kid and those hard fingers getting the knots out of my back, caressing my sore, wounded feet, was the first taste of what would later become a bit of an addiction. It was cheap, too, the equivalent of a couple of Aussie dollars.

Staying in a bungalow at Ko Samui, I swam, sunbaked and drank plenty of Mekong whisky. The beer was way more expensive so I had to make do with Mekong and Coke, which tasted a bit like rocket fuel. I drank it anyway and I made friends with other travelers, as you do, from all over the world.

One night we were drinking fast and hard after eating green curry for tea. I remember faces but not many names: there was a young married couple from Ireland, a youth worker from Germany and a couple of local young Thai men, including a striking 17 or 18-year-old boy. Sinead O'Connor and Bob Marley blasted from the cafe stereo as we drank and laughed the night away. It was 'good craic' as the Irish liked to say, and I thought nothing of wandering back to my bed, alone. Others were heading for the beach but I had drunk a bit too much and was ready to sleep.

Despite being unaccompanied, I never worried about locking doors. I felt completely safe on the islands, unlike in big capital cities in other parts of the world. I got into bed and felt a bit silly for calling it an early night. The fan above me was still whirring and the air was thick and humid.

Then there was a knock at the door.

Startled, I sat up in my T-shirt and knickers, thinking, what the hell? The boy from dinner appeared in my doorway.

'I come in?' he queried.

'Um,' I was caught on the hop. This was a new and unexpected scenario, even though I'd had some romantic dalliances while away.

'NO, no, thank you,' I politely declined, wondering what on earth had given this youth the idea that he might be welcome late at night in my room. I was 25 at the time, had taught in secondary schools for 18 months or so, and felt deeply that this situation was simply wrong, wrong, wrong.

'Why did you come here?' I finally found my voice.

'You smiling at me at dinner,' he answered. Yes, but I was pretty pissed, I thought but did not say. I felt flattered but dismayed and eventually had to tell him to go away.

'Okay,' he said. 'I no bother,' and obediently wandered down the lamp-lit path back towards the beach, like a naughty puppy that had been reprimanded.

I remember the feeling of gratitude that my beau (or stalker?) had been so easily dissuaded. Slightly alarmed, I then proceeded to latch the door. Not that it would really have made a difference should someone really want to enter the bungalow, but it made me feel a bit better.

The other memorable thing that happened was that I hooked up with a couple of male travelers, one from England, the other from Germany, Alan and Andreas. Alan was tall and skinny, smoked hand-rolled cigarettes and had very short red hair. All he ever wore was just a sarong around his waist. Andreas was German, olive skinned, stocky, athletic and funny. In a short while after we began talking the pair invited me to move on from Ko Samui to Ko Pha Ngan (or Koh Phangan), famous for its Full Moon Party at Haad Rin Beach.

I'd never heard of the tiny island, but as my new-found mates described it as beautiful, untouched, and far less touristy than Ko Samui, I was in. Whether I felt subconsciously safer with two male friends I'm not sure, but it was quite acceptable at the time to form new friendships quickly and easily. We caught a rickety ferry and it seemed to take hours to get to the island. Chatting on the way we worked out that our birthdays were on three consecutive days, Andreas on the last day of September, mine was on the first of October and Alan was on the second. Three Libras traveling together seemed fortuitous at the time.

On arrival I had enough cash to pay for lodging but that was it. I started to make inquiries about an automatic teller machine. Alan laughed at me, 'Didn't you read up on this place? It's cash only.'

Fuck!

I did the only thing I could think of in order to stay on the pristine beaches at Ko Pha Ngan and pleaded with Alan to loan me some money, just until we went back to the mainland. Alan declined, understandably, and instructed me to catch the ferry back, get some cash out, then return. He explained that if I did that, I would show commitment to being there with them and I would enjoy it even more. To this day I don't blame him for not lending me any money. After all, I could have returned to the mainland and headed for the airport.

What followed were two more interminable days of ferry travel before I could truly enjoy the last leg of my journey, with me cursing my own ignorance and the fact that no-one bothered to inform me that the island was so isolated there were no cash machines.

Funnily enough it wasn't until many years later that I realized that I hadn't really experienced a traditional Thai massage on the island of Ko Samui. A conventional Thai massage doesn't use oil. The masseuse follows 'sens' lines in the body and moves body parts through a series of yoga like postures. The masseuse sometimes uses their feet and presses and stretches the body. I discovered this when a new massage therapist arrived in a small country town in Victoria, of all places, and I was the only person who was game enough to request a Thai massage.

When I returned to Tullamarine customs went right through my luggage. I must have looked a sight, with braided hair and tanned skin after following the sun for six months. My parents said they didn't recognize me. I'd discarded the photos of my American friends snorting snuff in London; after all, I wasn't stupid. So there was nothing to fear except the ripe smell of my undies and the tattered state of the one pair of shorts I'd worn non-stop for the trip. I think I cried when they fell apart and I had to throw them away.

While I wasn't returning to Australia with a raging pill addiction, which afflicts many people who go to South-East Asia, I had developed a taste for adventure and for the good things in life.

Exciting but also ordinary events took place on my return: I had children, got married (in that order), renovated houses and taught English in a little country high school. Traveling had given me the confidence to move to the sticks and embrace a different life; one that I enjoyed away from the city, because of different friends, fresh sights and the great outdoors. The initial attraction was the small school, nearby surf beaches and Wilson's Promontory, and, of course, the partying. Country life has now become a part of me, or maybe the other way around.

One day when both my boys were in primary school and we were experiencing a heatwave (a highly rare occurrence in South Gippsland, a bit like Ireland), I hurt my shoulder while swimming at Waratah Bay. Duck diving under a wave, seeing the fizzy foam above my head, I swam through the clear, blue water below and OUCH! Something major had happened and that specific moment in time began a never-ending search to cure the pain I felt on my left side. Strained muscles, rotator-cuff injury, whatever. All I knew was that I had something wrong with me that was virtually unfixable.

Cue chiropractor appointments, massages, Reiki, myotherapy, you name it and I tried it. I even had a cortisol injection where the doctor had trouble finding the right spot guided by an ultrasound; what, did they miss the fucking lecture on giving needles at uni? I'd get relief for a while and a whole range of different diagnoses but nothing seemed to last for long. Eventually, cash poor, I'd be walking around with my left shoulder glued to my neck and in agony.

Since then I've had: a Swedish massage in my lounge room, a massage at the Great Barrier Reef, massage at a Bear Gully yoga retreat, a Hawaiian massage that resulted in a massive bowel movement (fortunately the therapist warned me this was one of the 'benefits'), I've tried acupuncture, had numerous chiropractor visits and myotherapy, a massage when I cried on the table.

Some people don't understand my obsession with reflexology, but it's never been anything sexual. Unlike Jerry Seinfeld's hilarious, iconic conversation with George, who said, 'It moved.' The only truly weird thing that's happened on the table is that a strange woman who was giving me a treatment thought I was menopausal – I was in my early forties and complaining about feeling feverish. I wasn't going through the change. I was getting sick. She kindly offered to…erm…stroke my nether regions, or said my husband could do it. Naturally I chose the latter and left as quickly as possible. This happened in Australia, believe it or not. Crazier sh*t sometimes happens close to home.

Recently I visited Vietnam with another teacher. An intrepid traveler, I shadowed him through the chaotic streets of Saigon, dodging mopeds. Anyone who has visited Ho Chi Min City will be aware that traffic light signals are optional, so pedestrians take their lives in their hands just crossing busy roads. Even when all the traffic does stop there is always one rogue driver who decides to keep going. It amazed me how good-natured all the beeping and giving way, or not giving way, was; it was organic. Miraculously, no-one ever seemed to get injured. In Australia there would have been road rage, lost tempers and fender benders everywhere.

In parts of Saigon where we were walking on footpaths mopeds came up behind us, either beeping their horns as warning, or politely saying 'excuse me'. That was all very well, I thought, except I never knew which way to jump, left or right, to avoid being run over. Nonetheless my instincts must have been good or I was incredibly lucky, because we walked all over the place and never once had physical contact with a moped.

You have to have a sense of humor to travel in Asia. Occupational health and safety is non-existent. From rat sightings in cafes to watching men and women working with jackhammers on city streets wearing thongs, one needs to travel with an open mind. Women shoveled gravel, whole families sat on motorbikes. Babies slept on their parents' shoulders on the back of mopeds, too. Wherever we went, or stopped, I took delight in simply watching passing traffic, marveling at how much could be transported on one small bike.

Peter explained why women wore long sleeve shirts even though the temperatures were quite high. Unlike myself, who politically incorrectly or not, loved the sun, Vietnamese women prefer to keep their skin lighter, as darker skin symbolizes the working classes. The women were dainty and elegant, the men, laid-back and cheeky, cigarettes hanging from the sides of their mouths. It was not unusual to see someone having a kip in the middle of the day, slumped over on the handles of their motorbike, noisy traffic zooming past.

We tried to eat where the locals ate and I developed a new-found passion for Asian food. Pho was the best food ever when I was feeling nauseous. (Pete ate crickets, because we couldn't find live coconut worms. I declined, due to a bad stomach. Neither of us spewed, but it was close.)

This trip was a bit different to being in Thailand, however. I had cash, lots of dong – there are 100 different dong jokes – and cash could only mean one significant thing – SPA TREATMENTS.

The Caravelle Saigon, had to be the poshest, most luxurious hotel I had ever stayed at: massive swimming pool, room service, rooftop bar, business center, beautiful Vietnamese men and women willing to organize a car or help with directions.

Although I initially felt a little out of place traveling with a backpack, the staff were so professional and the French architecture a visual treat so I soon got over any self-consciousness. On our very first day in Vietnam we walked to the river, saw the Ho Chi Min statue and surrounding gardens and experienced the chaos of Ben Thanh Market, Saigon's busiest central market. As advised, I kept my eyes down, for the most part, and ignored calls of 'you buy, you buy' from pushy stallholders. The wet market was mind-boggling. I couldn't believe the fish and meat sitting out of refrigeration. We decided to hold off purchasing souvenirs until the very last day, due to the fact that we had an overnight train trip from Hue to Saigon in order to fly back to Australia.

Jetlagged, because we kept waking up at 3 am Vietnamese time which was 7 am Melbourne time, I decided to go for some bodywork. It had to be done. My mate got up before sunrise every day in order to buy a pork bun for breakfast. I looked out for opportunities to have a massage.

At Kara Spa my feet were gently washed in water with rose petals in it. I lay on the table and the young female masseuse removed my robe. Beautiful classical music played and my senses were overloaded. Then, suddenly she was on my back. This was a new and unexpected development. Too tired to work out what was going on, or for that matter, fight it, I relaxed. A very petite young woman was crawling all over me giving me the most gentle and wonderful massage I had ever had. I don't know if I fell asleep but it was likely. The therapy was world class, and I happily paid the 90,000 dong, or 50 Australian dollars, to feel lively and refreshed, ready for the next escapade, sans jetlag.

My need for a fix didn't stop there. We walked miles around Hoi An by both day and at night checking out the sights and the markets, and my feet were killing me. Peter had been on a mission to find the Morning Glory restaurant to eat some stuffed squid. We'd shared lots of giggles over the innuendo, but when we did finally get there one night he was disappointed that the squid wasn't available, so we made do with pork, rice and salad. The next day, he was still focused on finding squid, so we proceeded to walk miles, eventually stopping for delicious bánh mì by the river.

Unexpectedly, the stuffed squid was procured in the less touristy part of town, in a family-owned cafe that faced onto the less crowded side of the river. I used the toilet and realized that we were actually dining in the garden of a family home, which had a motorbike in the lounge room.

I decided to go for a rubdown one 40-degree afternoon, to get out of the sun rather than go back to where we were staying and fall asleep. May, a few doors up from the Sunset Motel in the old part of Hoi An, gave a brilliant shiatsu-style rubdown for a lot less than what I'd paid in Saigon. My only concern was the see-through netting in the front window, but she waved away my worries, 'Don't worry, no-one look.' Once I was spread-eagled on that table, I truly didn't care.

And it turned out to be a bonus that I'd stopped and had a rest, because the realisation dawned on me when I returned to Sunset Motel, I'd lost my camera. It was merely a cheap Panasonic but it had my only photos of the trip on it. I'd taken some on my mobile, but the resolution would be lacking.

My mate insisted on finding the camera despite the fact that I'd initially suggested a night in, as we were moving onto Hue the next day and were pretty exhausted. That night we retraced our steps back around the ancient city of Hoi An, to the market stalls we'd been by that morning, the place we'd stopped for coffee and where we'd had lunch. The place was packed but luckily, he was tall. I followed along in the half-light, smelling the incense and pushing through crowds for what seemed like hours, without any luck.

As it turned out we never found the camera but it did not matter. It transpired as we returned that my tour organizer had been keeping himself amused by taking photos of me while I wasn't aware; sleeping on the plane, stuffing my face, drinking coffee. The more horrendous the photo the more amusing. He laughingly said that they'd soon appear on the whiteboard during staff professional development. I was mortified.

Can you ever have too many treatments? No, I'd argue. I was only in Vietnam for ten days and the last little splurge was on a facial. It was great. I knew I'd return with dewy, youthful skin. But, I have to say, I was still envious of my travel companion. He had his one and only massage before we headed to the airport and back to the dreary Victorian weather, school, and a flu epidemic. Too embarrassed to admit I would go for a third treatment, I had shown restraint for fear of embarrassment. I'd cut off my nose to spite my face.

Unfortunately, most ordinary people can't afford to travel often, so I have some advice. Do what I do. Take every opportunity for some time out. Going for a treatment is not illegal, nor will it break up your marriage. You get a natural high and sense of wellbeing. Whether it be eating Pho in Box Hill, or having some deep tissue work done at Blackburn North shopping center, I utilize every sneaky opportunity to do something for myself.

Recently, I found a little Chinese place in a nearby plaza, where you can just walk in for a treatment without an appointment. I told my son and husband that I had to do a 'big shop' and promised to bring them home McDonalds in order to throw them off the scent.

But hubby was onto me when I came home four hours later. 'What took you so long?' He asked, before his blue eyes twinkled as the penny dropped. I paused, guilty, mentally calculating an hour's drive there and an hour's drive back dodging wombats, the rushed visit to Coles for groceries, going through the takeaway drive through.

My face was flushed and I might have looked like I'd had a quick knee trembler somewhere. Luckily, he understood my penchant and did not begrudge me 'going for a rub'.

The single hour on the table, listening to Chinese music, and taking pleasure in the magical touch kneading out the bumps in my shoulders took me to another world. I pretended I was elsewhere, developed the outline for this short story, dreamed about my next overseas trip, and crazy sh*t in Asia – pure escapism.

Better still, if I had to do the grocery shopping, which I detested, why not do it floating on air?

CHAPTER 5

GRIN AND BEAR IT

Emily Saunders

I've often imagined what I'd ever do if I came face to face with a potentially dangerous animal in the wild. And due to spending a fair bit of time camping around Canada in the autumn during my early twenties, I'd given a lot of thought to my bear survival strategy. Would I lie down and pretend to be dead? Try and frighten it? Run downhill? I did see a couple of bears during my Canadian days, but they seemed more interested in eating the contents of the garbage bins stacked outside the ski resort I was working at, than snacking on me. Nevertheless, despite the improbability of occurrence, I have a spent a lot of time pondering the issue and researching exactly how it feel to have strips of skin gnawed off the back of your neck. At times like this I really think I need a hobby.

There's something about being eaten alive that both horrifies and fascinates. That possibility, once an issue for our ancient ancestors, is so far removed from most of our daily lives that we can give ourselves license to vividly imagine it, safe in the knowledge that it will most likely never be something we experience.

It was 2004, and I'd been living on the north island of Japan – Hokkaido – for about six months. It had not been easy transition from my former life in Australia where I'd been living a charmed life in the sunshine of Byron Bay. My days in this incredible part of the world, were spent going to the beach, hanging out with mates, partying at houses with pools on weekends, drinking smoothies, eating veggie burgers, and calling people 'sister'…all the usual activities. However, after a short season at the ski fields of Mount Hotham that winter, I had a taste for snowboarding and I'd heard that Japan was the place to be for serious snow.

It was relatively easy to get a teaching job in Japan in those days, the big English schools were actively recruiting all over Japan and they were not too picky. I'm sure any former student from this era could attest to that; teachers were often total knobs, and frequently stunk of a nostril tanging mix of alcohol, BO and Japanese energy drinks that were rumored to contain actual speed. Present company excluded I hope, although those energy drinks really did pick you up after an enthusiastic night at the all-you-can-drink karaoke bars. Public drunkenness is so accepted in Japan that intoxicated people lying in their own vomit are often looked on with a mix of hilarity and genuine caring. I once saw a railway station attendant gently patting a dude on the back who had chundered all over the floor in the railway station. Not only that, but he was sprinkling sawdust on the pile of last night's curry from a handy bucketful of wood shavings he happened to have on hand. Obviously, he was an experienced vomit cleaner.

But back on the north island of Japan. Life was foreign and isolating, and work filled my days and evenings. I knew nobody, outside a couple of the Japanese teachers at my small school and I was the only *gaijin* (outsider) in my building. On first arrival there was one other teacher living upstairs, hut he left a week later and kept giving me piles of junk he didn't want to have to pay to throw away. In the end I begged him to stop it, but then came home just after he had left, to find a final box on my doorstep that contained ten dusty video cassettes of *The Golden Girls* and a CD entitled *Loose Shoes and Tight Pussy*. Don't buy it by the way, it could actually be the worst CD I've ever heard. It makes Patsy Biscoe's *Christmas Hits* look like a cultural masterpiece. Once, when extremely bored, I tried to see what Dorothy and co were up to and the large amounts of dust inside the tape immediately clogged up my video player and busted it. Thanks a lot Jordon. Though when you decide to pop on a few badly recorded episodes of *The Golden Girls,* you know things the situation is pretty grim, and I really should have made an alternate afternoon plan. Sometimes on my days off, I literally would not speak to an entire soul or see a friendly face for 48 hours. Sapporo was not like Tokyo back then, foreigners were rare, relatively speaking, and almost looked on with suspicion. I did notice that the local bakery stopped displaying plates of free samples after I would religiously visit the day before my pay check and make a meal of the offerings.

But as all things seem to do if you persevere, life got better, and finally when I heard that a guy I met in Byron just before I left was paying me a casual visit that September, my levels of excitement went into overdrive. I'm a planner. When fun things are on the horizon I like to meticulously lock down a tight schedule of planned activities, yet present it as a casual and spontaneous option of last-minute fun that simply happened to happen.

Naturally I'd saved all my days off up and had a tight ten-day itinerary on the go. I'd been interviewing my students for months on their suggestions for adventures in Hokkaido during the autumn and visiting travel agents and collecting glossy Hokkaido booklets. It wasn't easy because everything was in Japanese, and I didn't have a computer, and therefore, access to the internet. But something had caught my eye; a series of hot water waterfalls and pools that you could lounge around in in a place called Shiretoko, a tiny peninsula on the far east of Hokkaido, said to be the last untouched area of Japan. The Shiretoko peninsula juts out into the sea and is a UNESCO protected slice of centuries-old Japan, separated from Russia by a small strait of water. The name Shiretoko itself means 'The End of the Earth' in Ainu dialect, which is the language of the native population of Hokkaido. You have to admit, it all sounds pretty enticing.

It was my mission to get there. My friend had arrived in Sapporo a couple of days before, and after taking him around the city and attempting to show off my Japanese, we jumped on a tiny plane and headed east. After an hour we landed in Nakashibetsu, where we hired a car and made the final hour-and-a-half drive to the Shiretoko National Park. It was an interesting experience just being that remote. No highway signs in English (navigating was a touch tricky), no English speaking at all going on in shops and cafes. We really felt like we were in the wilds.

The peninsula itself is incredibly beautiful. Rolling mountains, incredible forests and volcanoes shrouded in mist – it was real

Monkey Magic territory. I kept expecting Monkey, Pigsy, Sandy and Tripitaka to appear out of the forest in pursuit of a wind demon. (By the way, did anyone realize that the actor who played Tripitaka was actually a girl?)

Shiretoko is where you have the chance to see Japan as it once was, and it is astounding in its beauty all year round. We were there in late autumn and the colors of the trees were spectacular. During winter, the sea freezes and people go diving under the ice to see some kind of glowing underwater ice creatures called sea angels, which I still don't quite understand what the hell they are, even though I asked all my students about them scores of times (I was the master of small talk after a year of fishing for anything I could run with during drawn-out English conversation classes). The best description I can offer, is that they look like a living pink sea flower.

I saw thousands of salmon swimming up-stream, the rivers alive with the heaving mass of their thrashing, slippery silver bodies. And those hot water waterfalls were every bit as incredible as they looked in the glossy brochures I used to take with me on the train every morning. To get to them was quite something else as well. After a long drive to the end of a mountain road, we then walked on through the trees for a few hundred meters. And finally, we walked for 20 minutes up the middle of a warm, rushing river than ran through the middle of the forest. At the beginning of the river walk there were two young Japanese men renting footwear made out of coiled rope so that you wouldn't slip on the river floor. The water level never reached beyond our thighs, and it was much easier just wading up the middle than trying to climb along the rocks at the side. When at last we made it to the top, we could see all the hot water gushing out from tiny gaps in the rocks above. All of it pouring out from below the earth. As we climbed higher, the water got hotter and hotter until it scalded our feet, and there was a smell of sulfur in the air. Down below was the series of waterfalls with pools of hot spring water at their base. We could see other people closer to the bottom waterfalls, so we stayed high and had the top pools to ourselves. The water was so full of minerals that it felt slightly oily on the skin, and I'll never forget the magic of sitting there, surrounded by trees, the waters splashing down to each pool below in the descending twilight. Sometimes experiences are so beautiful that you feel like you've slipped momentarily into a fantasy.

I'd been hoping to spot a Japanese brown bear in this so-called 'bear hotspot'. Shiretoko is famous for its large bear population, and apparently 800 bears live in this tiny peninsula. But that evening it was not to be. The next day we headed for the other site of mass bear spotting, a series of five beautiful lakes. What we came across however, was about 500 Japanese tourists all dressed up in special hiking outfits. If there's one thing the Japanese love, it's to really follow through with an outfit. There are no half measures there. Rich or poor, security guard, taxi driver or teenager, every look is finished off with finesse. Bird watchers were in no short supply here either, and they all had their own look too; it included a matching shirt and pants, rubber boots, a bucket hat with a feather pinned to it, and a pair of binoculars around their necks. Meanwhile, all hikers were decked out in the usual hiking gear, plus they were carrying a special hiking stick and had a bear bell attached to their jackets. These bells are meant to frighten away bears, though between you and me they don't sound that scary. More annoying really. All you could hear at the five lakes were hundreds of different tinkling sounds. Forget the threat of bear attack, they were all in danger of me strangling them to death – anything to stop the tinkle tinkle.

After this no bear show I was getting a little mental and somewhat reckless in my endeavors to see my brown, furry intimidating buddies; from calling 'Here Beary Beary' out the car window at any possible bear habitat, to exploring dense woodlands on the side of the road. It was in this frame of mind – desperation mixed with an undeniable need to show off – that I suggested we abandon the car and take a little stroll up a roped-off former road that was now covered in tall grass and bushes and had a 'Beware of The Bears' sign at the entrance.

We began the walk uphill and after about a kilometer, we began to realize that the road didn't actually lead anywhere and that we were perhaps asking for trouble, deep in the forest at dusk in bear country. And autumn is when the bears are most active, searching high and low for food to load up on before the hibernation months. We began to shift uncomfortably as I suggested that perhaps going straight back to the car would be a good plan. We started to walk back down that kilometer of abandoned grassy road, liberated by relief that we could abandon the bear search and go back to our hotel for some sake and soba.

As we rounded a bend I saw something in the middle of the road about 20 meters in front of us. Holy shit, yes it was. A very large brown bear. It was on all fours and scrounging round in the grass. On all fours it came up to our shoulders, so it was a big bastard there was no denying it.

'It's a bear.'

I could hardly speak the words. My companion saw what I saw, and without discussion the two of us turned and bolted back up the road as fast as we could go. Unfortunately, we realized again that the road didn't lead anywhere, it was getting darker, the bear was between us and our car, and finally, that running from a bear was the very worst thing you could do if personal safety was high on your list of priorities. We stopped and turned around and waited for it to come round the bend in pursuit. It never came. Maybe it didn't see or smell us. Maybe it wasn't licking its brown lips and imagining the taste of human. But the question remained: what the f*&% were we going to do???

'Let's go stealth in the bushes,' suggested my crazy newly-beloved. I immediately imagined scenes of us lost in the dark being chased by a man-eater and all his rabid friends. Luckily, I had interviewed all my students about bear survival strategies during some particularly dry grammar lessons to break things up a bit. 'No,' I asserted, 'What we want to do is make some noise, the bear hears the noise and runs away.'

'Are you sure?' questioned my skeptical mate. I wasn't sure, I wasn't sure at all, but it was all I had, and there was to be no stealth of any kind. So, we prepared for the unnerving walk back to the car, as I let out the loudest wolf whistle I could muster up. I'm so glad I was one of the few to perfect that skill during my tender years. However, I almost expected the bear to respond like a dog and come bolting towards us. It was a tense wait.

It was such a bendy, overgrown road that every turn was terrifying, and all the while we were yelling, whistling and woohooing. I was singing an original number I like to call 'Please Don't Eat Me', while a particularly horrifying story about a bear attack my student Keiko had told me about was replaying in my head. Apparently, Keiko's grandfather and his friend ran into a bear in the mountains of Japan few decades back. They managed to make a run for it, but the bear stalked them and in the end attacked the friend. Apparently, it didn't eat the flesh of the unfortunate man, just sucked all the blood out of his half-alive body until his heart stopped beating. I decided to keep this particular tale to myself, which, anyone would agree, was a wise move. We got further and further down the road and still there was no sign of the bear. Where the hell was it?

Suddenly my companion said 'Look down! Look down!' I glanced to the ground beneath my feet, and there in the mud were the biggest bear footprints I'd ever seen. At that exact moment something whooshed loudly out of the bushes right before our eyes and scared the absolute bejesus out of the two of us. It was a mother deer and her baby going like the clackers. They bounced across the path and up into the forest above. We then heard a massive crunching coming through the dense scrub straight towards us and the call went out, 'Run, RUN!!!' I needed no more encouragement, it was bolt central, and we were off, every man for himself. My shoe broke mid-sprint, which made me last and primary bear fodder; it's hard to save yourself when you've got half a roman sandal dangling off your left foot. But at last there it was, we could see it at last! The car – the glorious car!

Out came the keys in the last 20 meters of the sprint. The doors were unlocked on the run and the two of us dove in and shut those doors tighter than my white jeans after Christmas dinner, and we both went into a sort of hysterical laughing attack. I can't even begin to explain the relief. I honestly felt like I had escaped certain death; well, at least a savage and disfiguring mauling. Nothing shuts down a romantic vacation quicker than being eaten to death. For the following three days, the two of us lived in a heightened state of adrenalin-fueled anxiety. Every time I thought about the incident, which was pretty much the whole time, my heart would beat so fast and I couldn't shake the feeling that running as fast as I could was the only possible solution to ease the panicked fear. It was the strangest feeling.

I later heard that during that particular autumn there were many more bear attacks than usual. Hungry bears were spotted lurking around kindergartens in eastern Hokkaido. While one particular town, in a desperate attempt to ward off these brown beasts and their relentless appetites, starting collecting acorns and storing them in big bins on the outskirts of town. Hopefully this strategy would lure the bears away, and satisfy their unyielding hunger. Let's just hope that the bears preferred the taste of these bitter brown nuts to that of the town's population of four-year-olds.

We left Shiretoko the next day as planned, and flew straight into Tokyo – from one jungle to another. My heart palpitations gave way to a joy of being alive, and desire to make the most out of every single amazing thing we did in that crazy city, which was later to become my home for three years. There's nothing like thinking you're about to die to really bring home the thrill of living. Or maybe I was in love. Or just maybe it was the shock of discovering bear-flavored ice-cream in the world's craziest ice-cream shop at Sunshine City in Ikebukuro. Whatever it was, it felt great. And bear-flavored ice-cream is a horrible concept, even worse than the snake flavor I also spotted. But apparently, it's better than bear in a tin.

No wonder they want to eat us too.

CHAPTER 6

THE HONORARY CONSUL

Ian Harris

'Ian, the simplest investigation by an amateur could identify GJ.
Czech Consuls are not too thick on the ground in Bali OR anywhere.'

In August 2002 I flew to Bali looking forward to a six-week working holiday, but life there was pretty good and I remained until October 2008. I might have stayed longer, but things changed suddenly through no fault of my own and I was expelled and forced to leave within 24 hours. This is the story.

After several weeks of holidaying, I met, and was recruited by GJ, the Honorary Consul for the Czech Republic, to create and run Bali's first cosmetic clinic. We would cater to the expat and tourist market in competition to the emerging market for those services in Thailand. I would be the 'Western trained doctor' and the face of the Anti-Aging Rejuvenation Clinics (ARC). It represented an exciting opportunity to set up Bali's first dedicated cosmetic tourism clinic and to live in Bali. I really never thought that it would eventuate as it did, just as promised from the outset except for two tiny details.

First, GJ was my nominal partner and second, my real partner was Ibu M, GJ's Indonesian wife.

The penny might have dropped the day I arrived, when GJ met me at the plane on the tarmac. We magically avoided customs formalities and I was whisked through the Consular/VIP/APEC line at immigration in seconds and pushed into a waiting BMW with Indonesian and Czech Republic flags flying (we were even saluted by police as we headed to GJ's 'consular residence' in Sanur). I'd had only two quick meetings with GJ over six months and decided that although he appeared quite mad in an eccentric, yet affable sort of way, he was, more or less, dependable. Notwithstanding any reticence I might have felt at the time, I invested US$25,000 for a 25 per cent share of ARC.

So, there we were at the consular residence, sipping wine from a cellar chock-full of fine imported reds. Over the course of the next few hours GJ told me that he arrived in Bali as a backpacker in 1972, one year before the arrival of electricity, intending to follow the 'kangaroo route' to England via Singapore, Thailand, India and Afghanistan. GJ never left Indonesia. He started up an English language school in a 'shop house' in Poppies Lane teaching English by kerosene lamp on a dirt floor. He lived above the school and within a few years created a number of schools throughout Indonesia and made his fortune. He bought mansions in Jakarta, an island off the coast as a weekend retreat, opened a restaurant called Batavia in Taman Fattihillah, the old quarter of Jakarta, before it became trendy. The restaurant soon became the most exclusive restaurant in Jakarta and the first offering European 'haute cuisine'. The restaurant displayed autographed photographs from well-wishers who had dined there. They included Mick Jagger and Jerry Hall, Bono, Bob Geldof and many others, including the first president of the Czech Republic, Vaclav Havel, and soon after they met, GJ, expat Australian, became the Honorary Consul for Bali.

I asked GJ if there was any competition for the expat/tourist cosmetic market and he said that the only one was a clinic called Miracle run by Indonesian locals and marketed to locals and expats but not tourists. As it turned out, a few days later I read the local expat rag *Bali Advertiser* and saw an ad for Miracle Clinics offering the usual range of 'fluff and puff' beauty services as well as botox and dermal fillers. I couldn't resist a naughty urge and I rang the *Bali Advertiser* and instructed them as follows:

'Hello, I'm Dr so-and-so the new western medical director of Miracle Clinic. Would you change next week's Miracle ad so that the last line in bold reads "If it's a good result, it's a Miracle!" They duly printed the new ad in the next edition!

I settled into Bali life in a hotel in Seminyak within walking distance of iconic Balinese cultural centers like 66 Club and Hu'u Bar.

Our target market for the cosmetic clinic was tourists to Bali and certain sections of the Bali expat community; mainly Australians but also Europeans, Brazilians and North Americans. To get an idea of our target market, you need an insight into the make-up of the Bali expat community. It was, to put it bluntly, mostly 'Desperate Housewives'. Almost every weekday morning you would find a dozen or so kijangs (cabs) with cowed drivers nervously waiting in the trendy cafe La Luciola car park in Seminyak for their employers to finish their eggs Benedict, soy lattes and perhaps just the one mimosa. Inside La Luciola you would have seen coiffed and peroxided heads through a cloud of smoke wafting from a hundred Marlboro Lights. You would have heard Fulham accents and Australian twangs discussing their husbands' many shortcomings (and short comings), the unreliability of the domestic staff and of course the bitchiness/dire financial straits/sagging bosoms of whomever among them couldn't make breakfast on any particular day.

The desperate housewives are busy: school run in the morning, three-hour breakfast with the girls, manicure, pedicure, massage, yoga, tennis lessons and all that before the serious business of shopping and afternoon sunset drinks at Ku De Ta! The next day it began all over again. 'Simply exhausting darlings!' The next cohort of clients, although limited in numbers, were The Very Rich. There are more very rich people in Bali than you would imagine, but they are rarely seen. They have very large estates in Canggu, Ubud and the Bukit but they would never lower themselves to actually slum it with other expats and tourists at Cafe Warisan. Instead they had a chef come to cook for them. Every so often they threw very large parties to which you might be invited; the most coveted, almost mythical invitations, spoken of in reverential tones. The Very Rich invariably expected to have their cosmetic procedures done at home: whether it was botox or a face-lift.

Next, coming a distant third, were the committee members of many organizations in Bali with various nominal activities and purposes apart from having lunch, taking down memoranda and awarding each other certificates of achievement. The nearly all-female committee members join in order to 'give something back to the Bali community' but instead of sending a check to Oxfam, they spent most of their time bickering over who should be on the subcommittee for membership rule compliance or who should be in charge of the tombola at the next Christmas party. They could usually be found having lunch at the Arena Sports Cafe in Sanur or Gracy Kelly's Irish Pub. For the sake of completing the picture, the expat community comprised small cohorts of our potential market.

The first expat community in Bali was started by Giancarlo, a near-mythical Italian trinket and furniture exporter in the early seventies. He and his friends were known collectively as the Trinket Trade Brigade (TTB). Its members were all tanned, slim, covered in interesting tattoos and dressed like hippies circa 1967. They survived (just) by sending one container a year of dubious trinkets, furniture and batik to a cousin's shop in Milan or Turin. They congregated at Bali Deli or Ku De Ta, where they nursed cocktails for incredible lengths of time. Legend has it that one TTB member, Franco Piccolo, managed to sip a Long Island Iced Tea over seven hours in 2000.

Then there were the consultants and technical advisors, the group to which I belonged. We were variously skilled people brought to Bali to impart real or imagined skills on the populace. They were mostly in the hospitality industry but included architects, lawyers and doctors. They wore their technical advisor badges with pride and a certain amount of entitlement, even if they were only once the fifth-assistant sewage consultant when the Four Seasons was built 20 years before and hadn't worked since.

Lastly, there were the undesirables: timeshare salespeople, aging former strippers, unemployed building contractors and their wives, 60-year-old Australian 'property developers' driving their mopeds to their rented bedsits in Poppies Lane, and slightly ill Dutch retirees and so forth, all in plentiful supply. (With special thanks to my friend and co-contributor for this guide, Nils Wetterlind who had to leave Bali, rather suddenly, so he could 'spend more time with his lawyer', as he put it.)

ARC clinic opened its doors for the first time on 1 September 2002 with a mandatory *keselamatan* or blessing given by the local priest. I discovered quickly, as do all expats, living and running a business in Bali differs radically from merely holidaying there. It is more an industry in itself dealing with the masses of regulatory authorities. Nothing is ever put in writing and you have to make a 'guesstimate' of what needs to be paid to what authority – always in cash. I was told that whenever the local government authorities came to visit I should lay low because if they suspected a westerner was involved in the business then the 'facilitation fees', as they were euphemistically referred to, might double.

To this day, I am unsure if the clinic was ever fully registered with the local health authorities, or any authority for that matter. I often asked the clinic manager if we were registered as a clinic and the answer was always 'still pending'. To make things worse, everything broke down on a regular basis: electricity outages at least once a week, slow or non-existent internet connections, fucked fax machine, unavailable printer cartridges and so on. It took me a while to get used to the fact that this was going to be the new normal for me. One morning, faced with broken everything, I lost it. I had gone in early to do some work online and send faxes. I didn't think there was anyone else in the building. The internet was down, the printer wouldn't work and there was no fax connection. I started yelling, 'this fucking useless computer, fucking fax machine…nothing fucking works in this country!' Then I heard a thud outside. I ran out to see our secretary on her back on the floor, the clinic manager stood over her and waved a hand fan.

I said, 'What happened? Did Endah faint?'

Christine, 'No it was the evil spirits.'

Me: 'What evil spirits?'

Christine: 'In you…'

The next day the priest was hurriedly summoned to perform another *keselamatan*.

I remember being woken up about 11 pm on Saturday, 12 October by two massive noises; deep-throated and palpable roars, separated by a few seconds, there was no doubt in my mind – bombs. I walked out on the balcony and saw a red glow in the night sky above Kuta.

Shortly after a friend rang me and said that a bomb had gone off at the Sari Club. He said people had been killed, he'd heard maybe eight but that it was total chaos and he'd get back to me. Fatalities totaled 188 and hundreds of life altering injuries. The immediate cost in human lives and suffering has been documented but the subsequent cost to the economy of Bali was long-term and devastating, especially as this event was followed by the start of the second war in Iraq then the emergence of Sudden Acute Respiratory Syndrome (SARS) in the subsequent months. This created a 'perfect storm' that rained down on tourism to Bali and hence the whole economy. After the bomb, tourism to Bali was virtually wiped out in 72 hours, the approximate time it took for nearly every tourist to leave the island. Owing to the subsequent events, no-one was going to come back in a hurry; a long-term catastrophe.

GJ reckoned it would be at least '18 months' before tourism to Bali returned to even pre-Bali Bomb levels. We held an emergency directors meeting. It was decided to keep the Balinese staff on, temporarily close the clinic and look at setting up another one in Jakarta, which was full of expats and would not likely be economically affected as much as Bali.

I returned home to Australia three month after I arrived in Bali wondering what would happen next. Certainly, GJ and the local directors seemed relatively sanguine about this disaster and confident of recovery. I too was sure Bali would recover, but wondered if I wanted to be there at all.

In the first week of January, GJ rang me and said that they had found a suitable location in Jakarta and when was I coming back? I blurted out 23 January, for no particular reason except to give me a couple of weeks to decide what I wanted to do. In the end I thought I should make the effort to see it through, and protect my US$25,000 investment. I returned on 21 January 2003 and we recommenced operating ARC Clinic. Over the next few years we opened similar clinics in Jakarta, Medan, Surabaya and, of all places, Makassar in Sulawesi. I could understand why we opened in Jakarta because of all the expats living there, (30,000 Australians alone called Jakarta home) but Medan in North Sumatra and Makassar in Sulawesi? There are no expats and very few tourists in these places. GJ said that he wanted ARC to appeal to more Indonesian locals not just the expats and tourists. So as it happened, we got crazy busy and six years flew by. On 23 January 2008, alone in my office, I trawled through the bank statements and noticed a transfer of US$30,000 to an unknown account. I asked the clinic manager if she knew about it. She said that Ibu M transferred the money to her account (Madame M, Indonesian wife of GJ and director of the company).

When GJ came to the clinic the next day I asked him about the money Ibu M had taken. He said that she had and added, 'That that's what they do.'

'That's what who do?'

'Indonesians.'

So, I made the decision to call Ibu M out on this and request that she return the money to the company account. It proved to be a near fatal mistake; I caused Ibu M to lose face *hilang muka*, the worst insult a westerner can do to an Indonesian.

On a particularly stormy night in 2008 at 11 pm Suntiani, my Indonesian wife and I were awakened by a knock on the bedroom door. It was one of the maids:

'*Ada tamu, pak!*' (There are guests mister!)

'Guests?' I was awake but uncomprehending. 'It's a bit late for guests.'

I opened the door to eight Indonesian men loitering in the living area of the house. One of them approached me and gave me a piece of paper.

'It's a search warrant...for drugs,' he said in perfect English. I scanned the warrant and noticed that they had included cosmetic creams.

'I'm the head of narcotics in Bali,' he said.

'What on earth do you want with cosmetic creams?' He didn't reply. 'This is a set-up, isn't it? How much did GJ or his wife pay you to come here with this search warrant?' All he said was that they were going to search the premises. I told my wife to ring her father.

My wife's stepfather was a General in the Jakarta Police Force, although neither the head of narcotics nor GJ could have known that. My wife rang and filled him in. A few minutes later she handed the phone to the laconic DEA head.

There followed a series of punctuated '*Ya pak siap*' (Yes sir) before he returned the phone to my wife, who then said her goodbyes and hung up. I asked my wife what her stepfather had said. She replied that we had to search the police officers before they searched the house. I noticed at this point that two of the officers slowly retreated into the background darkness. So, there we were, my wife and I patting down Bali's finest and getting them to pull out their pockets, take off their shoes and socks (the shoe was on the other foot now I mused) and even checking cigarette packets, as per orders from Jakarta.

After the all clear they proceeded to do a very desultory search of the premises but still insisted on taking four large box loads of cosmetic facial creams. After about only ten minutes the top cop said to me, 'There are no narcotics here. We will leave now.'

By 'we' he meant 'him'. The remaining cops insisted on hanging around, as they do, and started playing with my wife's guitar and singing. (Another friend who had a similar experience said the police hung around for hours playing with his three-year-old son's toys.)

I asked my wife how to get rid of them. She said that they were probably hanging around for a drink and money (the age-old Indonesian police custom of *mencari uang*). I said, well give them some tea and then tell them politely to fuck off. She said that she couldn't tell them that so I left the somber officers and went back to bed, much to the annoyance of my wife.

About 30 minutes later, another police officer turned up and I had to get out of bed again. He was talking to my wife and, after a few minutes, I asked her who he was.

'He's a detective.'

'So, what does he want?'

'Money, I guess.' Great. Now we had to entertain another cop.

He beckoned me to follow him into my bedroom, followed by my wife, put his arm around me and started giving me a lesson in basic Indonesian.

'*Ist'riku?*' (Your wife?)

'*Ya ist'ri saya.*'

'*Ist'riku,*' he said, correcting my grammar.

Then he started talking to my wife in Indonesian. She informed me that he was going to take the cases of cosmetic creams and wanted my passport. I had no choice but to give it to him. He then wished us good night and left.

Fortunately, the other cops took this as a sign they should leave also, presumably as their boss was now leaving. None of this made any sense to me until I asked my wife what else he said. She said he suggested that I get legal advice. I said, 'What for? They didn't find anything.'

'*Mencari uang,*' she replied with a sigh.

Next day I saw a lawyer who didn't write a thing down (except his bill) and told me he would have an answer.

'Answer for what?'

'Facilitation fee,' he said.

'Ah, *mencari uang,* right?'

'Something like that.'

'But I don't care if I get the creams back; they don't even belong to me. They just got dumped here by that psycho GJ.'

'Yes, but you want your passport back don't you?'

In the end I had to pay a 'facilitation fee' to get my cosmetic creams back. I tried saying I didn't want them as I was returning to Australia anyhow but it was made clear that return of my passport was conditional on paying; it seemed the police didn't want the creams either.

POSTSCRIPT

My father-in-law later sent two of his men from 'Intel' in Jakarta to find out what happened. They stayed with us and were happy (as in smiling inanely) when they confirmed that GJ had rung the police and told them that the creams were full of methamphetamine. The police then said that they could only be bothered searching the house if he paid them $2000, which he did. They also added that as the drug bust ploy had failed, GJ had also paid another $2000 to have me deported.

'But the good news is,' they beamed, 'that if you pay another US$2000, you can stay!'

I had no intention of getting into a tit-for-tat fight with a deranged, rich expat and his equally deranged Indonesian wife. In any event, we had planned to return to Australia; by that stage I'd had just about enough and wanted to get out of Indonesia.

I had to pay the Jakarta officers' costs and was told I had to give them a present. When I asked my wife if they wanted more money the answer was no, she said.

'No, one of them likes your surfboard in our room.' It was an old surfboard and I was more than happy to get rid of it. The last sight of them was watching them walking out of Denpasar airport with one of them, in full uniform, carrying a 7-foot surfboard. I occasionally wonder if he ever used it.

One week later my passport was returned. I opened it and there was a red stamp giving me 24 hours to leave the country.

CHAPTER 7

THE THAILAND 25TH ANNIVERSARY TRIP TO HELL

Kerrie Atherton

We were so excited about going away for our 25th wedding anniversary! This was especially exciting as it had been about five years since we had last been on a holiday. After a long time struggling financially we had finally saved enough and THIS was going to be the trip of a life time! My hubby had only ever been to New Zealand (if you can even call that going on a holiday overseas) and to Europe in winter on a work trip so he was feeling really pumped about this trip. Our first REAL OVERSEAS HOLIDAY YAYYY! Plus, a celebration that we had stayed together for 25 years. Since he was a kid, he has been absolutely obsessed with the sun needing to be out and shining in order to have a good day, so sunny Thailand – well, so he thought – would be the perfect location. Time alone with his wife, eating gourmet Thai food, massages by the beach, hours spent basking in the sun in the tropical paradise by the pool and staring out at the beautiful blue ocean were what he had dreamed of each day in the year leading up to the trip.

Little did hubby know that he would be lying by the pool in the rain, battling flooded streets, nearly have his back broken, babysitting a Greek widow whose family had left her on her own because they were attending to her grandson who had dared to pat a wild cat on their first night at the resort and was suspected of contracting rabies. He would have seven sleepless nights due to the Japanese tourist invasion on either side of our room, four days and nights of chronic diarrhea and end up in hospital the day before we were due to go home! Not to mention the many arguments when I kept going over to the phone on his side of the bed to call security because there were some sort of spa-bath parties going on next door starting at midnight and lasting until 3 and 4 am three mornings in a row. And then to top it all off he had to deal with a manic-depressed sleep-deprived wife! Well, let's start at the beginning, when we were still in the dreaming of a wonderful holiday and great days ahead.

Day one. It had been a long flight. My husband, who is not much of a talker and not really that interested in what someone is having for breakfast, took one for the team and sat in the middle seat. What could be so bad about that? Only the fact that he had someone with verbal diarrhea sitting next to him who wasn't really that interested in sleeping. Eventually, after they had knocked themselves out with a few drinks, the conversation stopped and he got some sleep. We got off that plane thinking we would smoothly transition to our next flight but there was a severe storm and we all had to get out and walk in the rain for some distance to our next plane. Eventually we were strapped in and on our way for our one-hour flight into Patong. The excitement was growing. It was midnight and we were very tired and expecting to quickly get in a taxi and arrive shortly after. But there was a very long line waiting for us and then over an hour in the taxi. When we finally arrived, exhausted, we crashed on the very hard bed and woke up needing a massage the next morning.

Day two. We headed out to breakfast and almost immediately noticed a little massage hut on the beach in front of our hotel. As soon as breakfast was over we were down there. We were told to take off our clothes in front of about five other people and there were no change rooms; we refused the offer of going nude and kept on our underwear! I was happy with my massage therapist, who looked a bit experienced, and then my hubby's came around the corner. She was extremely large and I thought that was fine as she would have strong hands and he likes a firm massage. After relaxing for about ten minutes I opened my eyes and turned my head to talk to him and saw a horrifying sight – she was walking on his back, hanging onto a rope attached to the roof of the hut! He looked at me with terror in his eyes and I thought, if that rope snaps he will be airlifted to hospital. Afraid for his safety he hurried the massage up because it was actually hurting him and he feared that he could end up with a broken back.

After the massage we headed to the pool to recover. Hubby was relieved that he had survived and we relaxed and lay in the sun. We then ate lunch and stayed there for the afternoon, feeling somewhat blessed. Something we love doing is eating out at nice restaurants, and the restaurant on the water at the hotel looked divine. After going back to our room, we got all dressed up and headed out for our romantic dinner. It was a smorgasbord. The only problem was that none of the food was hot! We were somewhat cautious and hardly ate anything, but hey, the atmosphere was great and it was romantic, so two out of three ain't bad. Then we met the Greeks. Me being a counselor and such a friendly compassionate person couldn't ignore them once they said hello and told us that they were there for a family wedding and that it was off to a bad start. Their inquisitive young son had patted a stray cat, which bit him, and they had spent the day at the hospital because the doctors were concerned he had contracted rabies. Then to add to their difficulty, they had their mother there on her own because her husband had passed away a few months before and she was very depressed. Well how could I just walk away then! So, I spent the next two hours embroiled in a type of a counseling session and then excused myself because my husband and I were very tired as a result of the jet lag.

After getting two extra padded blankets on our bed to make our beds softer, we attempted to go to sleep. Two hours later we were woken to loud doors banging and someone on the balcony next door screaming in Japanese. After 20 minutes I went out and motioned to the screaming woman that we were trying to sleep next door, and I attempted to go back to sleep. Then for the next three hours the Japanese guests on either side of our room liaised back and forth to each other's rooms, in and out banging the doors every time, and then they proceeded to run spa baths on and off for three hours. After calling security four times things settled down and at about 4 am I finally got to sleep. We woke up the next morning at 8 am and my husband, who had slept intermittently through the noise the night before, was ready for an early breakfast, but I was not. Being convinced by my husband that I could sleep in the sun by the pool after breakfast I headed out with my costume and towel. After breakfast we settled down by the pool and then I hear the dreaded words come out of my husband's mouth: 'It looks like a storm is coming!' Knowing that he was there for the fun in the sun holiday, this was already starting to feel like hell.

Well, when you can't have fun in the sun on holidays, I guess the next best thing is shopping, right? Well, yes, except when you're in a taxi and then it starts pouring and then the roads start flooding. So, most of the afternoon was spent inside taxis and stuck inside shops waiting for taxis and arguing about what to do next. Eventually we got back to the hotel, saturated and cold. We ate dinner then thought we would get an early night. The Japanese had been warned the night before that they would be moved if they started up again so they were on their best behavior for night two.

Day three. The sun was out. Celebration time! We were headed for the beach. Planning to stay at the next beach along for the entire day, we started our long walk to get there. We were literally ten minutes down the road and who do we bump into? You guessed it. The Greek grandmother. She said, 'Thank goodness I have bumped into you today because my family have all gone out for the day and left me on my own and I am so lonely.' What could I say? Certainly not, 'Have a good day see you later,' but 'Well would you like to join us?' I thought she would say no, you two have a great day together, but she said YES. So, off the three of us went to the beach for the day. She had no money either so that meant we also paid for her; her drinks, her massage, and also her lunch. She had a fabulous day! We consoled each other with the fact that we had done a good deed, and we told ourselves we could go to the beach tomorrow (even though it ended up being the only sunny day at the beach the whole holiday).

That night was as bad as the first, as the Japanese partying ramped up to a new level. We had been told though that they only had one night to go so we knew we would be able to sleep on night four at least.

Day four. Phi Phi Island. Woke up tired! But the adrenalin was kicking in. Every single person we encountered said 'you have to go to Phi Phi island'. What everyone told us was that when you arrive there is a beautiful banquet smorgasbord lunch waiting on the island. I thought, 'Wow! This is going to be the highlight of the trip!' Me being the eternal optimist, I had been trying to look for the positives in every day even though we were feeling so disappointed at what had happened on the holiday up to that point. I was more than convinced that the last four days of our trip would come good. So, we arrive at about 10 am and were split into two groups of people. There was a storm brewing so it was at the discretion of the drivers as to whether the boats would even leave or not, and then we were even given a warning: go at your own risk. Whatttt?!

We were in the second group, which I thought had to be good. So, the first group are loaded into a fairly big boat and off they go. But we don't have the kind of gung-ho confident driver that they do. And he can't decide whether to leave or not. By this time two hours had gone by and half the people had decided not to go at their own risk and had gone home. Still optimistic, we waited. Finally, at about 1 pm we headed off, but in a very small boat with about 12 people on board. I loved sitting up the front and there had been no warnings given that if anyone had back or neck issues they should take extreme caution and sit up the back of the boat. So, I headed straight to the front and as the waves picked up and we headed at high speed along the choppy water, I was being catapulted all over the place. And then the boat started thundering sharply up and down, up and down, with each time it hit the wave shuddering my neck with full force. I was literally hanging on for grim death wondering how on earth I could get to the back of the boat, because I had neck problems before getting on the boat and I didn't want to leave with a broken neck. We stopped, as all the boats do, at a beautiful spot where the Leonardo DiCaprio movie *The Beach* was made. The driver said we could all dive in for a quick swim as we were on a time schedule, which I later found out all depended on being able to get back home due to the weather conditions. I skipped the swim considering there was a thick film of petrol all over the top of the water from the multiple boats that stop there every hour. Our quick swim however was delayed because of a couple on board; she was wearing a full burka so couldn't go in, but her husband decided to go in and he didn't know how to swim. All of a sudden, we heard yelling and he was starting to drown. So next thing some of our guys were on a rescue mission to get this very large guy back on the boat. He was okay, just extremely shaken up and highly embarrassed. I was absolutely starving by this point and it was nearly 2 pm. All I could think of was getting to the Phi Phi Island to eat my lunch.

We had finally arrived. I literally ran off the boat and lined up for my lunch. My heart sank when I arrived with my plate and there was barely any food left. The heat candles under the bain-maries to keep the food hot had gone out and there were no staff left to bring any more food. Lunch was over. How could this be? Where was my smorgasbord?! There was cold rice left, some bowl of sauce stuff with a bit of floating seafood and some kind of vegetable dish. Extremely cautious of food poisoning after the many warnings from tourists who had visited Thailand, I said to my husband, 'Do not eat the seafood.' We were like ravenous dogs. So what does he do? He eats some of the leftover floating seafood! For the next couple of hours, I just couldn't wait to get back. Stuff the beautiful scenery and the nice beach. I felt like I was on the TV show *Survivor*. We had a quick swim, went to the prehistoric toilet in the ground and climbed on the back of the boat, homeward bound.

The driver wasn't so chatty this time as we hopped on board. He looked a bit concerned. I wondered what the heck was going on now. Then he said it, 'We are heading into a storm. Strap yourselves into your seat belts and life vests and don't move. STAY IN YOUR SEATS.' Then we started off. I was absolutely terrified. I knew the trip was about an hour back and he started handing out seasickness tablets. Our small boat was being thrown around like a rag doll. Water was coming in the back of the boat. The waves were about 4-feet high all around us and I was praying my little heart out hoping that we would get back alive. Then, all of a sudden, the boat stopped. We had broken down. My anxiety levels rose to new heights. Eventually, after what seemed like an hour (it was really only about ten minutes) we were back at high speed, bang bang bang on the waves, headed for the shore. We finally made it. I was absolutely shaken up.

It was pouring with rain and we had to get back in the shuttle to head back to the hotel. It should have been a 20-minute trip but the roads had started flooding from the torrential storm that had hit. We'd already been on the bus for about half an hour when my hubby announced he needed to go to the toilet. I said, 'Well now there is nowhere to go!'

Fifteen minutes later, he said 'I am busting, I need to go!' After an hour we got off the bus and he ran to the toilet and was on there for about 20 minutes with chronic diarrhea. I said, 'I told you not to eat the seafood!'

Hubby said 'I am sorry I feel too sick I'm going to bed. You will have to have dinner at the resort on your own'. I really hit a new low. I was so depressed I just wanted to go home. I was stuck in a dodgy hotel, on my own, I knew no-one, not even the Greeks were there now because they were all off at the wedding festivities, I had a sick husband, plus it was flooding. I felt so alone. My hubby told me he would be better the next day so not to worry. I had some consolation in the fact that the Japanese maniacs had checked out so I knew I would be able to sleep that night, but as it turned out my hubby was up on the toilet about 20 times and was violently ill.

The next day he was too sick to do anything so he told me to go shopping for the day. I ate alone that night as well.

The next afternoon, hubby, convinced he had just had a 48-hour episode of food poisoning, came out for dinner to a local Thai place in town, but only ate rice. He told me he couldn't stand the smell of Thailand or Thai food anymore, but we were stuck there for another three days.

The next day we at least did some shopping but he was still not feeling well. He ate something, his first kind of meal, the next night and then was back on the toilet all night. The next morning was spent at the hospital getting medication to try and get him better. While we were at the hospital I couldn't help but feel concerned that he might not be better in time to go home. I saw some very sick people there and felt grateful that the Thai hospital system was running like clockwork. It actually gave the Aussie system a real run for its money. While we were there we saw a girl pushing a guy in a wheelchair and the doctor told us about them. They were a couple who had gone over on their honeymoon and he had been knocked off his motorbike and was smashed to pieces and they were stuck there for weeks. At least we were not in that position!

We were starting to really celebrate the fact that we were going home and were counting the hours before we left the country. Another full day of rain and eating on my own and we were out of there. The night before we left we bumped into the Greek grandmother and she came up to me with tears in her eyes as she thanked us for our kindness towards her. That made me feel happy, that at least something positive came out of it. Maybe she was the reason for our whole trip!

Anyway, that is the conclusion of the twenty-fifth wedding anniversary Thailand trip to hell and we are NEVER GOING BACK. The poverty over there really distressed us and taught us to be so grateful for the blessed kind of life we have in Australia. We were so happy to be back on Aussie soil. On a side note, it was a year before my husband ate Thai food again!

CHAPTER 8

FORBiDDEN LAND

J 'Momo' Mordant

In 1950 the Chinese People's Liberation Army invaded Tibet and seized control, and it remained essentially 'closed' to the outside world from then on. It was a crucial strategic zone between the mega powers of India and China. They called it an 'autonomous region' which was political jargon for 'it's ours, but let's pretend it's not'.

Then in early 1985 China started to allow a trickle of trade and tourists to enter Tibet from Nepal, through the spectacular mountain passes of the Himalayas, across the so-called 'Friendship Bridge'. I was blessed to have slipped through that opening like a cat burglar in the night, right before that window of opportunity slammed closed again and was nailed tightly shut.

I found myself in Kathmandu in the spring of 1987 and several freaks I knew had already trekked off into the mists, but now China was refusing to issue any more travel visas for this overland route. It had been a convoluted affair at best, involving telexing to Beijing to request permission to apply for a visa, awaiting their response, transferring money to their bank, sending off applications, etcetera. So, my trusted travel companion, Ozone, and I crafted our own. This was before the days of Photoshop, and 'cut and paste' was a manual operation with Xerox being our only high-tech ally. Ozone was a tall, dashing, Clark Gable-esque artist with piercing blue eyes that could see right through you (and indeed were often focused somewhere far, far away) who had a keen sense of adventure and a penchant for the ridiculous, an epic explorer of the road less traveled, and one of my best friends. Since an early age I had super lucid dreams of monks and monasteries that I only discovered were of Tibet much later on. 'The land of clouds' had a special, almost mystic, familiarity, and now it was beckoning palpably to me. We sent off our applications, while many others who were applying along regular channels were being refused, we were somehow granted a visa!

That was the easy part.

In the early morning rain, we were sardined into the bus together with a variety of livestock, luggage and a generous Asian excess of bustling people, and headed north-east from Kathmandu up towards the border, resting at roughly 2300 meters above sea level. Hours later, we came to a rude halt somewhere around the town of Tatopani, the last village before the frontier as, somehow, the road had come to an abrupt end. Well, actually, it had slipped off the side of the mountain into the Sun Koshi River, and the mountainside and path onwards were a rushing molten mudslide, a mucky bubbly mousse with boulders the size of our bus skidding down its side. It was really quite an incredible sight; a liquid moving mountain that groaned with the sound of the debris it was carrying along. Our adventure had come to a premature demise.

We spent the night huddled under tarpaulins around braziers that were fueled by yak shit, drinking aromatic chai while the wind whiplashed the plastic walls. In the first grey light, we took our backpacks to the edge of the mudslide. There was some kind of way across and people were dragging themselves through the mud one at a time, like forging a fast-flowing river. It looked absolutely terrifying, but it was the only way forward. I watched for a while, and then I saw someone leading a horse with big saddlebags across. The horse had huge panicked eyes and was resisting, pulling away, and the next moment it was gone, swept away down the slope, his head emerging far in the distance. I don't know if he survived or not. Taking my balls in hand, I ran through the molten mud, stumbling and dodging tree trunks and rocks to slide, exhilarated, across and onwards towards the 'Forbidden Land'.

Guarding entry to the 'Roof of the World' were a group of fearsome Chinese soldiers. Clad in the obligatory green drab Mao suits, sporting high heeled Chinese slippers, with constant cigarettes dropping ash carelessly, these scowling and shouting scions of the People's Republic brandished their weapons with a camp fervor. It was somewhat comic, but with a tangible air of hostility, as they shouted questions angrily at us. It was make-or-break time. My heart was pounding audibly. The idea of having to return across that treacherous mudslide and maybe following the fate of that wild-eyed stallion certainly was not appealing. Then, somehow, miraculously, they stamped our 'visas' and waved us impatiently out of their way. We were in!

Keen to put a little distance between us and the border, we flagged down a cargo truck and hitchhiked on to the next village of Tingri, our first real taste of Tibet. There were heaps of military convoys on the narrow road, and we had to pull over for lengthy periods to let them pass. Tingri was set on a huge expanse of open grassland, with buildings on each side of the road like a Wild West cowboy town. We were welcomed into a small family home. The kitchen was dimly lit by butter lamps and filled with medieval-sized cauldrons, and butter churns. There the shy mama introduced us to the wonders of tsampa, ground barley flour, which was a little powdery unless mixed with yak butter tea. This 'tea', with floating balls of fatty oil (yak milk has about twice the fat content of cow's milk) actually tasted, and smelt, like rancid butter; it only became a little more palatable when thought of as mushroom soup. It wasn't the tastiest, but refusal would have been rude. Then there was chang, the local fermented brew; cloudy, a little fizzy and all too easy to drink. In the morning we gave our hosts postcards of the Dalai Lama, which were forbidden at the time for political reasons. They were like currency. The family were overjoyed and hugged us as we set off to Chomolungma, as the locals call Mount Everest: the highest mountain in the world, closest to the heavens, a place of pilgrimage and home of the Gods. It was supposed to be a fairly easy three-day walk.

The first day was a long, eight-hour hike as we meandered gently upwards to finish at a small huddle of temporary tents, made from parachutes and held down with rocks, sheltered from the wind, where the nomads grazed their yaks. Yaks are incredible, especially up close. Something between a bison and a woolly mammoth, massive with shaggy dreadlocks and sharp horns, these had pierced ears and prayer flags sewn into their manes…they are the Tibetans beast of burden, suppliers of milk (butter and cheese), wool, meat and fuel from their desiccated 'droppings'. The nomads were beautiful people from Kham in Eastern Tibet, tall, proud with long braided hair, high sunburnt cheekbones and bright eyes; they made us welcome with tsampa and many 'kettles' of chang, singing songs into the night in the flicker of meager firelight. The following morning, they directed us onwards to the next camp, pointing up a valley and around an escarpment. It was a beautiful day in amazing nature, so we naturally decided to try some incredible edibles recently purveyed from the famous Psychedelic Eric.

We had an amazing day, laughing at the multiple sun-bows dancing around the peaks, absorbed in the minutiae of alpine flowers and giggling glacial streams as we continued ever higher, the air growing thinner as the majesty of the view over the high plateau expanded to a seemingly endless horizon. We were children dancing carefree; little did we know how drastically that was about to change. It's questionable whether our diet helped with our inner compass, but as the day started to fade, in the gathering gloom, we came at last to the promised nomad camp. Slight problem; nomads, by their very definition, move, and the ones we had counted on spending the night with had done just that. There was still the remains of a hearth, and a circle of stones where the camp had previously been, but a distinct absence of either man or beast. We were all alone, ill-equipped and unprepared, on the side of Mount Everest at over 4000 meters with the light and mercury dropping fast. Suddenly, it wasn't quite so funny.

I put on all my clothes to try to keep warm. No fancy alpine accoutrements, no thermals, just some colorful trippy silks and a Nepali sweater. We piled the stones to make a little windbreak. There was no wood to burn, being already high above the tree line. I didn't know if we'd survive the night. We passed the hours cuddled up together for body warmth, eking out what rest we could. Luckily, the weather didn't turn foul, and come morning we were still kicking, although somewhat feebly, slightly sore and somewhat sleep deprived. Then we had to decide whether to continue onwards, or to turn back down the way we had come. You might think that the way onwards would be simple – the highest mountain in the world, just set the sights to the top and head off. In reality, being high in the mountains, there are endless false horizons; you can't actually see the peak if you're too close. On the one hand, it was supposed to be just one more day of trekking, on the other we really had no clue as to where to go and were in no condition to continue. Naturally, we decided to continue.

We spent the whole of the next day trying to gain altitude and aiming for what we imagined was the top. The air grew thinner as we climbed higher. After just walking ten steps it felt like I had run a marathon. I had to stop and rest frequently, panting. We were tired and irritated and started arguing over which phantom track to take onwards. In the afternoon, an ominous deep noise made me jump out of my reverie. Across the valley we had just painstakingly traversed, the whole side of the mountain seemed to be sliding down in slow motion, groaning and rumbling. It was a small avalanche. I felt humbled, and moved to tears. I was just a tiny creature inching across this vast and majestic terrain. As the day wore on, I was getting more anxious and tensions were starting to mount between Ozone and myself. As the sun dropped dramatically on that second night, Ozone spotted a little natural indent in the mountainside and we decided to take shelter there. We ate the last of our tsampa sullenly, just mixed into dry unappealing balls with a little icy stream water. It was the end of our food. I wanted nothing to do with Ozone by now, his complaints and worries, but we were forced to cuddle up together again for body warmth.

In the morning, Ozone wanted to head back down. He was running a temperature and the glands in his groin were swollen. I wanted to continue up. I was sure we must be close. I coerced him upwards with frequent stops just to catch our breath. My head was aching from the thin air. Then Ozone collapsed, complaining that he just couldn't walk a single step further. His glands were apparently infected, on top of the lack of food, the altitude and the uncertainty. 'Just leave me,' he said melodramatically, like a character from a classic adventure movie. 'Go on without me. Tell my mother I love her.' I was really tempted. I was impatient to keep moving rather than being slowed down by this spineless hypochondriac. Maybe I should go ahead and look for help. We sat for a while in the audible silence. I imagined I could hear bells. They seemed to be getting louder. It must have been the altitude. Then, like a mirage, a man appeared on the mountainside above us. He was a lone nomad with a solitary yak; very unusual as they normally travel in groups, but he had had some issues with his posse and was heading down on his own. Not willing to let him out of my sight, he led me around a couple of escarpments until I could see the fluttering of prayer flags in the distance.

Rongbuk is said to be the highest monastery in the world at a little over 5000 meters. It is nestled in a glacial valley dominated by the pyramidal peak of Everest in the background, the highest point on the planet, rising nearly another 4000 meters above us. It was truly 'breathtaking' and a bit otherworldly, but I was overjoyed. The monastery itself had an air of desolation. Apparently, it had been almost totally destroyed by the Chinese in the 'cultural' revolution during the seventies. The monks there were a bit of a contradiction too. I had always thought of Tibetan monks in lofty spiritual terms, but these were unreasonably greedy. They are given plentiful Western food supplies and equipment freely by departing expeditions heading down the mountain, and they just sat there smugly in Gore-Tex and fleeces demanding exorbitant prices for the most basic of rooms. I pretended to be a Hindu pilgrim and did the final approach barefoot, clad only in a thin lunghi, but the monks were not impressed. It's not as though we had too much choice. Sure, there were also some small caves in the mountainside that had been used for meditation over the centuries. A lumpy mattress and a stinky blanket was my choice, total luxury! Just knowing that we were again connected to humanity, even by the frailest of threads was a total relief. We had made it to base camp alive.

Our glory didn't last long. On the second night there, we met up with some other freaks who had some amazing hashish they had smuggled in from India and we all got completely high. In the middle of the night we were stricken by a severe case of the munchies, and finding a stash of wood, cooked up some porridge and made some Tibetan fry bread with jam. We sat around the fire much of the night, telling tales and laughing. Come the morning the monks were not too pleased to find their wood stash severely depleted, and when we refused to pay their incredible prices, they chased us away, throwing stones and shouting what I imagined to be the loftiest of swear-words. The descent was considerably easier than the way up. There was a track of sorts, and we even managed to hitch a ride on a horse-drawn cart with a totally inebriated local, who fell disarmingly off his mount on several occasions, with the cart sliding dangerously near the edge.

We arrived in Shigatse right in time for a massive festival at Tashilhunpo monastery, the home of the Panchen Lama. He had spent ten years in Chinese prisons, and was the most important lama in Tibet, totally adored by the people, who had flocked in from as far away as Mongolia. They were dressed in their finest colorful clothes and weighed down with heaps of jewelry, braided hair set with fist-sized chunks of amber, necklaces with red coral and with turquoise headpieces coming down their backs, smiling wrinkled eyes, burnt cheekbones, they were really a joyous sight! Tashilhunpo was one of the only monasteries to survive the desecration of the Cultural Revolution, and is the largest religious school in Tibet. Amidst the droning of the huge Tibetan horns, punctuated by the staccato of the skull drums, monks in masks were cavorting around enacting archetypal dramas, entrancing the crowd. It felt like a cross between a festival and an invocation; there was a palpable mystical presence amongst the revelry. Then down the front face of the monastery, maybe 25 meters high, a massive thangka of Shakyamuni buddha was unfurled, brocaded and full of intricate detail, shimmering in the sun.

Leaving Shigatse we traveled through to Gyantse in a bus that was more like a cattle truck. This was where Ozone and myself were to part ways. I wanted to head down to Bhutan, the Land of the Thunder Dragon, along roads that were officially closed to all except for the Chinese Liberation Army. The borders of the tiny Himalayan kingdom were in dispute with The People's Republic. The restrictions made the journey somehow even more enticing to me. Ozone, however, was more enticed by the prospect of a young German girl he was supposed to meet in Lhasa. It was hard to say goodbye. We had bonded deeply over the weeks and had been through so much together, but we each had a separate path we wanted to take. He continued 'on the bus' while I waved a four-ton truck down and gesticulated for him to take me south, which he did somewhat reluctantly. After a few hours bumping along under the canvas in the back, he pulled over and came to a halt. I peered out of the back. It was an army checkpoint. My heart raced. I had no time to hide, and nowhere to go so as they flung open the canvas, started shouting, and dragged me out, pointing guns and prodding in an increasingly alarming fashion. They weren't joking. I was taken to the command tent. They detained me, locked up in a small room with a couple of soldiers who chain smoked and played cards abusively. The following day an officer came who spoke some French, and we managed to communicate a little. This wasn't just a case of traveling down a forbidden road, they thought I was a spy! I had no idea what they would do. They were a law unto themselves and I had no-one to call on. I wasn't feeling good, and now the situation had become critical.

The following morning, it seemed they had come to a decision. They had decided to dispose of me. They put me on a truck back the way I had come. I apologized profusely, and thanked the officer for clearing up 'the misunderstanding'. They even gave me some salty noodles. But I wasn't prepared to give up so easily. I now knew where the checkpoint was. I jumped off the truck as it went slowly up a winding pass and scuttled quickly off to hide amongst the rocks until I couldn't hear his engine any more. My stomach was feeling really weird. It had been for days already, but now it intensified. After eating, I had cramps in my belly that would double me over with pain. I thought it must be the altitude or something, maybe parasites, and when I discovered blood I dismissed it as being merely hemorrhoids, or maybe they had poisoned me? However, my resolve was intact. I really wanted to get to Bhutan! I walked in the mountains for hours. I was sure I had skirted the encampment, but suddenly I heard a gunshot, followed by shouting. Four figures in green drab uniforms were heading towards me, gesticulating. I stopped. They took me back to the camp again, where the officer was really not happy. He took my passport and told me if he saw me again he would have me shot. Bhutan was not to be. The following day I was once more sent off, this time with an escort, and my weary compliance.

I reached 'The place of the Gods,' as Lhasa was known, tired and dirty. More than a month had passed since leaving Kathmandu. I checked into the Banakshol hotel, the only place that foreigners were allowed to stay according to Chinese controls. I sighed with relief when I saw in the registration book that Ozone was already there, and as I mounted the stairs I could hear his laughter echoing around the inner courtyard. All the freaks that I had met on the road plus other familiar faces from Nepal were there hanging out, packing chilloms and getting stoned in thick clouds of smoke. It was a veritable freak brothers reunion.

However, although my spirits were high, my body was emaciated. I was persuaded to get checked at the local hospital, where they told me I had amoebic dysentery. I was severely dehydrated and needed to be put on a drip. It was time to rest up a little.

The hotel was fairly basic, but it had the best toilet in the world, where out of necessity I spent considerable time. It housed just a small crusty slit in the floor and had a little paneless window, but from here I could see the majestic Potala Palace perched on a nearby hill in its full glory. A little aside about sanitary mechanics in Tibet (after all this is 'Crazy Sh*t in Asia'); in small houses you generally have to climb a wobbly ladder onto the wattle and daub roof, where you deposit your contribution through a crack in the floor. Not everyone is a crackshot! This falls down to the room below where it is available to the pigs or cattle for recycling.

Freaks would hang out on the flat rooftop with its clean high air, impeccable views and strong sunlight, blasting a few tunes with cassettes on a boogie box...well, yes, it was 30 years ago. A kind of flea market sprung up. Some had traveled across China with collections of silks and bright cloths, others from India and Nepal with woolens, Hill tribe silver, Uighur tapestries; there were antiques, prayer wheels, knives, gemstones, haircuts, tarot readers. Others had restricted recreational substances, which blissfully, the Chinese seemed not to understand. We started making cheesecake from yak yoghurt strained through cloths, set over ground-up Chinese army ration biscuits, flavored with whatever we could improvise with: limes and ginger, apricots, jam, nuts. Our freaks chewed it up with fervor in their munchies.

It was party time! We managed to put a little sound system on the roof. There was a tangible sense of community amongst the travelers, who had all come from faraway lands to this little magical oasis.

We walked around the Barkhor Bazaar, and visited the Jokhang temple, the most sacred place in the whole of this sacred country. It dated from the seventh century, and pilgrims came from everywhere just to visit this venerable site. Some wore knee pads and padded mitts and had traveled prostrating themselves all along the route, often hundreds of miles. They would lie down full length on the ground, regardless of dust or mud, and then stand up and pray, walk forward one step and repeat the process as an act of veneration and purification. The Jokhang was where Padmasambhava was said to have magically overcome the earth demoness. A giant two-story prayer wheel gently stirred the air, thick with incense and the smell of yak butter oil being burnt as candles. It hummed with the devotion of centuries like the engine of some cosmic machine. I loved the buzz.

We stayed around Lhasa for more than a month, with little side trips to places of interest. Picnicked in the Summer Palace grounds by the lake, and visiting the Potala Palace, Sera and other monasteries nearby. It felt like home as we became more familiar with the friendly people and the ancient place. My strength returned and I felt revitalized.

How little did we realize that this dreamy, idyllic 'summer of love' was about to face a sudden and terminal winter of discontent.

It was late September and an autumnal crispness was in the air. There had always been a tension between the spiritual Tibetans and the martial Chinese, and our sympathies were clearly with the Tibetans. Then something snapped. There was an illegal political demonstration that led to riots, and suddenly the whole situation escalated, with the local police station being burnt. We could see the smoke from the rooftop of the hotel. I was told it wasn't safe to go outside, which naturally piqued my curiosity even more. But then there was a sound of gunfire, and excitement turned to nervousness. There was an intense army presence everywhere; soldiers, trucks and even tanks. I was told that the army had opened fire on a group of people by the Jokhang Temple.

Abruptly the army appeared at the hotel and rounded-up all the foreigners. We didn't know what was going to happen. They demanded that all of us leave immediately. They were not being patient, and they were armed. We were bullied onto waiting buses. Someone had their video camera smashed, another had his films seized. An English friend was not happy with this and started to argue, but a rifle butt silenced his complaints.

From the safe distance of Chengdu, we heard stories of monks and nuns being dragged from temples and being forced to perform humiliating acts, and accounts of civilians being tortured and killed. On attempting to get our fake visas extended for the fifth time, they were revoked, and we were told to leave the country within two weeks. We decided to head onwards through restricted countryside towards Burma to try to escape through the Golden Triangle into Thailand down the Mekong... buts that's another story.

Chinese occupation of Tibet continues today. A new puppet Panchen lama was selected by the Chinese authorities instead of the reincarnation found by the Dalai Lama and his team. Many Tibetans have been killed, others sentenced to death. The total number that have disappeared or been imprisoned is unknown.

CHAPTER 9

MY INDIAN BAPTISM

Leila Hall

It's probably good to start at the beginning of my very interesting relationship with India. You see, we didn't start off well, me and India. In fact, safe to say that I have never had such a chronic relationship with any other country in my entire life. We did go on to mend it later – but much later, and those chronicles will follow.

But for now, let's stick to the facts of my first trip back in 2003 when my work asked me to attend a conference in Mumbai. Being the adventurous type and loving to travel to new places, I enthusiastically obliged, having never been to India before. I traveled alone without any colleagues – just the way I usually like it. My mission was to assess the viability of India as a new market entry for our business, and along with the conference, I had lined up several meetings with senior business leaders in the financial services arena to assist in the evaluation of this market opportunity. Yes, it was serious stuff, and I was most excited and flattered that I had been chosen for the task. Alas, it was soon to be rendered to something quite different altogether, but I get ahead of myself.

So, I get to Mumbai all well and good, ready for the onslaught of India of which I had been warned many times. I mean, I lived over 20 years in Africa, so am pretty confident nothing can surprise me. I'm game for adventure and cultural diversity, and proceed to conduct myself as I always do when I travel – get out of the fancy hotel and into the real stuff around me. I had arrived the day before my work commitments began so I had some time to 'take it all in', so to speak. (Not long after, I was 'letting it all out' if you know what I mean!)

I always believe 'when in Rome…', so I decided to head out and enjoy some local culinary delights to be found in less-than-stellar premises nearby. Not quite a restaurant of Western standards to say the least, but I think we have become soft over here, so decided to 'get on down' with the local fare. It was a good sign that I was the only *gora* ('whitey') in the place, so knew I was onto an authentic Indian casual dining experience. I noticed several rats outside the restaurant, but it didn't put me off, as I assumed rats were just part of street life in India (which they pretty much are).

Later that evening, I was walking around seeing some of the most heart-wrenching sights of my life. The poverty, human cruelty and suffering I witnessed that evening had me crying over the phone to my husband back home. I just needed to off-load some of the misery and sadness I witnessed, and had no-one around to process this with. So, he comforted me and encouraged me to head back to my hotel and get a good night's sleep. Good advice indeed. My busy schedule of meetings etcetera started the following day, and I needed to be fresh and well rested to get through the next few days. Mmmm…

Rest? A tad. But later that night, I was writhing around in the most excruciating pain in my hotel bed, awoken by stomach cramps that felt like someone was trying to manually extract my stomach from my body. Of course, this was followed by an entire night of not knowing which end to put over the toilet first! Luckily the toilet and bath were conveniently co-located so that I could reach each with the relevant orifice simultaneously – a 'concert' of sorts! Mozart – not even close! This continued into the following days. I was in no state to make any meetings or conference without shitting myself or vomiting adeptly over anyone within 5 feet. So, I holed up in my hotel room for the rest of my time in India.

I called housekeeping and asked them to kindly drop off some clean sheets, towels, disinfectant and headache tablets outside my hotel room door. 'No madam, we will make up your bed and clean your room.' It was a five-star hotel after all! No bloody way in hell I was letting anyone into that room while I was still breathing. If I crapped out my final breath in that hotel room, well so be it – then they would find the atrocity within and there wouldn't be anything I could do about it. But not until it was literally over my dead body!

So, my anticipated business trip to Mumbai consisted of a few hours roaming the streets, eating truly local fare (none of the Western hotel food for pussies!), wailing over the phone to my husband, and then spending three long days in a hotel room that were beyond description – begging the Lord to put an end to my misery; any way He preferred was fine with me at this stage. But a shitty, smelly death in Mumbai was not to be my fate. I was finally able to gather the little strength I had left, and got myself, somehow, on the plane home. Luckily by that time, I only had enough left in my failing body to sleep, sleep, sleep, and my fellow travelers, still to this day, have no idea how lucky they were. There was simply nothing left to make its way out of my mouth, nostrils or ass! I'm sure I saw an organ or two frantically escape from my body in those deep, dark hours; at least I think that's what the big bits were that were hard to squish through the plug hole. And my head was pounding so hard I was sure my brain was about to seep out of my ears.

And so, when I returned home and regained my health, which took several weeks, I remember distinctly saying to my husband, 'There's not any amount of money they could offer me to move to India. If they want to open an office there, fuck 'em! Someone else will have to do it, and ideally they should be severely obese and in need of some extreme colonic irrigation.'

But man plans and God laughs. Only about two years later we were living in India – yes, living there! We had moved there with my husband's job, two small kids in tow. The kids were one and three, and if they could survive a year in India, they would be as tough as nails! And as for me, I was sure that I would be fine. I developed a strong immunity on that first trip. Not so much the immunity to that monster bug I contracted, but more of an immunity to feces – literally everywhere! Baptism by India, with a distinct stench and brown hue. India, bring it on! If you can't beat 'em, join 'em! And so, the Indian chronicles began.

CHAPTER 10

KO PHA NGAN CATASTROPHE

Piers Fisher-Pollard

Crazy sh*t and South Thailand seem to be as analogous as grilled tomato and melted cheese or PlayStation and cannabis when it comes to my experiences over there. It's as if it were the universe's master plan: the two were always destined to eventually complement one another, and like those tomatoes and cheese; though it can get sticky, it usually seems to find a way of concluding in some sort of agreeable fashion.

A veteran of many protracted stays I presently hold the tally of one rateable motorbike accident per holiday and can't resist the gorgeous islands in the less touristy Gulf of Thailand, notably Ko Samui and the diminutive Ko Pha Ngan, which despite its comparative slightness packs way more punch than its weightier neighbor. Ko Pha Ngan; an enchanted wonderland where you can lose or find yourself in a staggering variety of ways. A compact but rugged island with abundant white sand beaches and bays and temperate water serenely lapping the shore, steamy tropical innards and steep, jagged mountains surging up to 800 meters above the bays and crystal-clear water below. A drawcard for international travelers, not tourists: people who cruise around the world following epic parties, heavenly eclipses and planetary events, kicking around carefree on shoestring budgets. Ko Pha Ngan is notorious for its extraordinary full moon parties 13-odd times a year, hosting anywhere from 10 to 30,000 revelers depending on the season.

Tucked away down the south end of the island, accessed via a scarifying rutted dirt track that traversed an abrupt and enormous mountain in the middle, Haad Rin is a beautiful curved bay with rocky headlands blanketed in lush grass and coconut palms bracketing each end and a stretch of fine white sand with the languid water creating a constantly variable transition from land to sea. Bungalows, bars and open-sided nightclubs back straight onto the beach, where you can buy the local beer Singha or a wine cooler bucket of ice with myriad straws protruding like a bloated sea urchin, into which you poured a quaternary of original recipe Red Bulls and a three-quarter liter bottle of Sang Thip whiskey or Sang Som rum, both tasting identical, offering the exact same buzz and a unique and completely unclassifiable hangover.

Haad Rin is actually two beaches on a slim peninsula facing opposite directions. But the one everyone wanted to be at, and which hosted the parties, was Haad Rin Noi, also known as Sunrise Beach.

If you wanted to stay on the Ko Pha Ngan peninsula for four months, like I did, you had to make arrangements, because for those 5 or 6 days bracketing the party out of every 28 the demand for accommodation far exceeded its capacity.

The businesses along the 800-meter stretch of Sunrise Beach collaborated come party night. Normally a row of independent bars and clubs; they grouped together in blocks of four or five so their PAs were playing the same music and you could walk along the beach until you found a style or vibe you liked. The DJs were international names from all over: Ibiza, London, Berlin, New York, dishing out music from deep house and techno to progressive trance or ambient chill, and the local chemist stores put signs out the front proclaiming 'Full Moon Medicine Available'. They'd sell you anything legal or quasi-illegal: dexamphetamine, codeine, cold and flu remedies, benzos and these diabolical home pressed pills called truckers that cost about five dollars and just one kept you on your feet for 24 hours.

In such mayhem, where the industry and lifestyle is monopolized by the 28-day party cycle dictated by the moon and attended by a random and motley combination of drop-ins from all around the globe, I found that there's not only more to do than party, but also an endearing generosity of spirit in the souls who make up the contingent of locals that only reveals itself on certain specific occasions.

This particular trip was already different; it was the mid-nineties and I was there to challenge myself in a very different way from the trippers and partygoers, attending an event at a Buddhist monastery, Wat Kow Tahm, perched high atop the mountain that split the island in two. Every month they held a ten-day meditation course, ten days of absolute silence: no talking, no reading, no writing, no eye contact, no food after midday. Westerners were drawn in from as many places as those who came for the full moon parties. They came to study, grow and learn, or like me a little of each and a lot of just for the hell of it: another experience, perhaps finding a way to tame the monsters that lurked within and muffle the monkey-mind that is the modern undisciplined brain.

We were woken at four each morning by 108 jarring tolls spaced about two seconds apart from this enormous bronze gong that hung from a sturdy hardwood frame at the top of the monastery's grounds. The gong-ringer role was a voluntary task assigned at the beginning of the course; the challenge had been embraced by a pale crew-cutted German youth who was totally all-in, striking that gong with such gusto that I'm sure by the end of the retreat, after smashing that timber mallet into that bell 1080 times, there couldn't have been a trace of anger left in him.

Silent, every day. Routine. Sitting mediation. Yoga meditation. Breakfast. Sitting mediation, walking mediation. More sitting meditation, lunch. Don't enjoy your food, just chew it and swallow it. Attachment will only lead to loss and misery, feel nothing.

Despite the cautioning I couldn't help but enjoy myself, the monastery was a fascinating place; the food delicious, the energy palpable and the sights and sounds a treat. I'd sneak off after I'd completed my chores to spy on the monks chanting, or walk to the top of the property, the apex of the mountain. I could see all of Ko Pha Ngan cloaked in an emerald carpet; millions of coconut palms interfused with the deeper olives and jade of the rainforest plant and tree species. Craggy rock promontories and picture-perfect white sand beaches in a slow dance with the water all around, starting with the gorgeous pale celeste and aquamarine of the shallows, transitioning to catalina and baby blue as the seabed dropped, till eventually in the distance that bold, deep azure of the open sea shot outwards to every horizon. Beneath me magnificent sea eagles rode air currents like gliders, occasionally performing a few languid flaps to regain altitude or switch to a different stream before resuming their stiff-winged waltz with invisible forces.

'How're you doing, matey?' Process, Piers. That's Rodney the English guy with alopecia, and he's talking to you.

The course had been tough, more challenging than I'd ever imagined. From 40 beginners, half were gone by day three. Day seven was the next heartbreaker, even though you knew there were only three days to go it felt like you'd been there a few months and still had another to endure. Half again quit that day, so that only nine of us emerged intact out the other end. Rodney was one of them and one of the few I'd met before we'd begun. Talking was complex at first, but it all came back, along with a thumping headache in no time. Rodney wanted to meet up at Haad Rin and rent motocross bikes, spend a day exploring the island. I told him I planned to spend a few days at a quiet beach further north to process the course and we organized to catch up at Haad Rin in four days.

For the first two days I was a magnet. People sat next to me on the beach, stray dogs lay nearby. Birds twittered as I showered and strangers followed me and sparked up conversation anywhere, about anything. Feral cats congregated on my balcony as I slept in my cabin at night and rainbow-colored fish gravitated towards me as I swam in the aquarium-like sea.

But from the moment I was back on the loose, holiday mode resumed; drinking in bars, smoking the local cigarettes that appeared to contain ground up particle board and shoe-soles, and as always happens on Ko Pha Ngan, being offered suspicious looking rollies by strangers that contained fuck knows what and generally left you numb or speechless, or both. So, after two days the magnet's allure evaporated and the fauna left me alone once more.

The beach I stayed at was long, straight and sparsely populated. At the north end was a collection of around a dozen timber cabins grouped around a bigger structure that served as a restaurant, bar and hangout joint with backgammon, chess and an assortment of board games, every night screening two pirated movies on a large projection TV. They'd write the night's movies on a sandwich board and I marveled at how there was always a spelling mistake in the title of each movie: Tue Lies, Natural Bron Killers, Dumb and Dumper. Was it really a mistake or were the Thai owners rising to some challenge to maintain consistency?

At the south end was the bar at the end of the beach, a good 15-minute walk. It had cozy oversized daybeds and commodious comfy hammocks and was usually frequented by around half a dozen patrons. I never heard it referred to by any other name and it was run by a three-quarters crazy American expat called Zippo who'd been there since the Vietnam War ended. Nor did it have set trading hours; when the bar was open a bright orange lamp burned, visible all the way from the other end of the beach. When Zippo felt like closing for the night, he'd switch off the light. Sometimes, already laboring with a half dozen Singhas permeating through your brain, you and a solid temporary friend would be halfway there when off went the lamp; time to turn around and start the trek back homewards.

'You want motocross? This one, Yamaha, best brand by far. 125cc two-stroke, 300 baht. Very good, nice color.'

'Too small. Do you have a 250?'

'250 two-stroke Suzuki, very best brand lucky color, yellow not blue. Four hundred baht.'

That was about 20 Australian dollars. A lot of money when a beachfront bungalow with daybed, hammock and ensuite bathroom was half that and a good meal came in at a couple of dollars, but well worth it in the scope of things.

'You make a deal for two?'

'Sure, 800 baht. Passport please,' he held out his hand.

Thailand. They didn't give a shit if you held a motorbike license or had even rode one before. Show me the money and give me your passport; bike gets trashed and they sell your passport to some fugitive or charge you three times the repair costs, either way it's a victory. All over the island you'd encounter guys and girls with bloodstained bandages wrapped around their hands, knees, elbows and ankles; ninety-nine times out of a hundred it was from a motor scooter or motorbike accident.

Rodney and I had hooked back up at Haad Rin and I resumed my accommodation in a nice twin-bed bungalow set away from the noisy district; two futon beds, veranda with daybed and hammock and a rudimentary ensuite bathroom with super-luxury flushing toilet and a shower that you had to hop around in to get wet. The basics of life are fundamental really, it felt as though I were living like a king for 12 dollars a day. A local guy, Somboon, worked at the central restaurant, chill-out lounge and pirate movie theatre and we'd had some lively nights out; veterans of several disheveled 5 or 6 am homecomings.

There was a nightclub with a vast, open-sided dancefloor that held easy 500 people and one evening around 7 pm when the patrons were just getting boozy but still too stiff to dance I asked the DJ to put on the Monster Mix of 'Insomnia', by Faithless. A great track that ran nearly nine minutes. I loved having the enormous dancefloor all to myself and used every bit of it in a whirling, twirling freestyle interpretive performance, so that of course by the time I'd finished there'd be half a dozen to a dozen people dancing and within another two songs the dancefloor was packed. The simple law of attraction.

The next evening, I asked for the same track again.

'You like this song, hey?'

'Fuck yeah.'

The DJ wised management to my ability to get the crowd up and dancing and I was offered an informal position; four or five nights a week I'd dance to my song then for the rest of the night I got free beers. I couldn't see any negatives in the arrangement and they were happy too: the perfect win-win.

'You want helmet? Easy, only 40 baht. Good helmet, best model.'

The fact a helmet with a rental motorbike was an optional extra was disturbing in itself but hardly anyone wore them anyway. Rodney and I rode off on some pretty serious machinery wearing just shorts and sandals, Rodney's patchy thickets of long black hair trailed like banners in the wind behind him. We rode along the beach on the island's west side; it was hard going as the sand was wet and the wheels sank in, but things got harder when a feisty dog took umbrage to the noisy gadgets transgressing his personal space, running at my side as he tried to take hold of an ankle. I sped up, the tyres battling with the soft sand, to encounter a row of beached fishing boats with ropes stretched up towards the tree line. It was either Fido's fangs or a rope around the handlebars; somehow, I fended off the dog and dodged the ropes until he grew bored of me and went after Rodney, tipping his bike over and pouncing on his foreleg as if it were a rabbit about to flee.

The dog was retrieved by its owner, an old Thai fisherman who cursed at it and threw a stone from several hundred meters with alarming accuracy so that Fido went yelp as Rodney screamed help; we righted his bike and Rodney tried to garner sympathy by showing me the bite marks on his calf.

'That's nothing, look what I got from a monkey,' I said, showing him a festering wound on my right forearm.

'Matey, you ought to see a doctor for that.'

'Yeah, yeah, let's get off this fucking beach.'

We rode inland and soon faced the mountain; the track was steep, rutted and intermittently sandy and wound left and right and every direction in between. We both had a few good cracks at it, either running out of forward motion as the back wheel churned up sand and dirt or coming to an unceremonious stop, dropping the bike on its side and sliding back down until it came to rest. Regroup: we sat at the bottom and contemplated the challenge.

As we pondered how to get up the hill a Thai motor scooter taxi buzzed around the corner. The rider, in his mid-forties, had a bog-standard 125cc step-through with a tourist riding tandem and an enormous backpack strapped onto him. He rode past with the scooter gunned at full revs and stood up, leaning well forward over the handlebars as he picked a circuitous route up the mountainside,

139

sticking to the clay and dodging this way and that like a prize fighter, and Rodney and I took it in as he guided that kitten of a machine, loaded well beyond the manufacturer's recommendations, up the mountainside as though he were negotiating an inconvenient speed hump.

'Well, fuck me.'

We waited as a four-wheel drive SUV pick-up, the standard Ko Pha Ngan taxi, came down the hill horn blaring the whole way, skidding and sliding under brakes as the driver deftly negotiated the dusty slalom run. It always amused me, the Thai fatalism: they'd never slow down on blind corners, instead resigning themselves to the notion that if was their time then it was their time, the only concession to inviolability being to pin the horn button continuously as they sped around the bend. All good, as long as there wasn't another vehicle speeding in the opposite direction and also with its horn blasting.

The handlebar trick worked well, along with a vague recollection of the scooter rider's route, and somehow, we got our specialized all-terrain machines up the same slope as the overloaded urban motor scooter and were soon enjoying the pleasures of the plateau that made up the middle part of the island. The track branched here and there and Rodney and I stopped at a junction to discuss which route to follow.

'Race you down this one,' Rodney said, pointing to the left fork.

'You're on.'

Rodney took off and once again I marveled at his punctuated swathes of hair dancing in the wind. He braked for a corner and I shot past him on the inside, hitting the back brake and skidding through to get a good exit angle and pegged the throttle. I'd done a bit of dirt bike riding as a teenager and Rodney was tentative so I put some good distance between us. Two-stroke engines don't have valves like a four-stroke; they're rattly and noisy but pound for pound have a lot more pep, and when you reach a certain rev range they go into a manic stage called powerband. I hit it, the bike wailed and kicked its tail as it came on then took off like a dog shot up the arse.

This was definitely getting interesting, I was eating up the straights and drifting through corners like a pro, just as it occurred to me that I'd never been down this track before. Twenty-twenty vision in hindsight; I hooked through the next corner and squared Mr Reaper right in the monocle as ahead of me a deep hole jumped into my path, a rock the size of minibus behind it. Shit, where the fuck did that come from?

Skidding and sliding the bike ran out of ground and for a brief moment I was suspended, like the coyote chasing the roadrunner when he runs off a cliff, then physics caught up and the bike flew in an arc, headed straight for the rock. Everything was in slow motion, I could see the detail in the rock, some kind of basalt, stratified layers of slag, no that was sand sediments, how did they get in there, an ancient river bed? As the bike slammed into the rock I lunged from the foot pegs and actually did a vault – was that parkour? free running? – no it was just plain arsey, from the top of the rock, skinning my palms in the process before flying once more through the air, feet forwards and face up, to land skidding on my back along the gravel track for about 50 meters.

I stopped, complete stillness. Head still operational, good.

Systems check. Nothing appeared broken, no serious gashes or injuries. The back of my torso, arms and legs appeared to have lost about half of their skin as if I'd slid along a cheese grater, but by the time I heard Rodney's bike come around the corner I was already laughing like a maniacal Bond villain, still flat on my back. I sat up as he pulled to a stop.

'Holy Jesus fucking crap, look at your back.'

'I know.'

'Why are you fucking laughing, you mad cunt?'

'Rodney, you've no idea how close I just came to departing the planet. That was intense.'

'You're a crazy fucker,' Rodney propped his bike on its stand and helped me up. Yup, some deep scrapes and a fair bit of real estate of raw and bleeding flesh but otherwise I was peachy.

'You won't be able to lie on your back for a fucking month, matey.'

We retrieved my bike, very good best brand lucky color yellow; it wasn't looking the luckiest or the best. The forks were bent, the handlebars sideways, the clutch lever snapped and dings and scrapes all over, but it looked like a doable project; perhaps with a bit of reno work I could ride it back home. We used a rock to coax the handlebars back into their general position. The front wheel was back a bit but still cleared the frame. I rotated the brake lever back upright and tried it; no front brakes. But I could still pull the clutch in by its stump, so I hopped on and kicked it in the guts and lucky color best brand lived up to its namesake, the engine coughing and blowing a bit of smoke. A few revs and it was running pretty sweet; I took off slowly and it wasn't so bad.

No more racing but still good transport, so we explored more trails and came across a lookout where we stopped and took in the magnificent vista and beautiful day. Beside us was a tin shack made from haphazardly joined sheets of corrugated iron and strapped lengths of timer, holes cut into the walls for windows. Next to it sat a small Honda generator and a massive satellite dish, about half the size of the shack itself and mounted on its own concrete slab, pointed somewhere up at the heavens where a geostationary satellite must've been providing the occupant with celestial entertainment. Thais sure loved their TV.

I walked over to look at the dish, by far the biggest I'd seen in any domestic setup, and a middle-aged Thai man emerged from the shack. He wore cotton fisherman's pants and no shirt, a vivid scar running from his stomach to his chest.

'Nice dish.'

'Fuck, what happen?'

'Motorbike, bang.'

'Fuck man, go to hospital.'

'No, I'm fine,' I pointed at his scar. 'Same same, crash?'

'No, get parasite from the water, big worm. Chop out. Go to hospital you crazy man, you look fucking bad.'

'You get good TV from this thing?'

'One hundred twenty-seven channels. Have decoder, watch all free, US military satellite for navy bases. Most crap but see good movies and soccer game.'

'You have a car out here?'

'Sell car, buy dish,' he gestured at it and broke into a broad grin. 'I go now, Germany versus Hungary. *Sawadee khap.*'

'*Sawadee khap.*'

'And go to fucking hospital, you crazy farang.'

Rodney and I kicked around, explored a few pathways that led through the lush bush and found a mountain stream where I washed out my wounds, wincing as tendrils of blood joined the fast running water like fine, red threads before clouding in small eddies then dissolving away so the water became clear as fine glassware again.

We lay in the sun and debriefed about the monastery, Rodney saying he'd hoped the meditation would help him control his alopecia as it was stress related. It turned out he was an actor, as most are yet to be discovered, and was planning to visit Australia next. I asked where and he said Bondi Beach, just about every traveler's go-to destination; I said cool, I live there, we should hook up. The afternoon was getting on so we decided to start making our way back to the south end of the island.

By the time we got back to the top of hill the sun was low, and already, pinky orange smudges painted the horizon. My best brand lucky color motorbike was behaving well and both of us were riding like the little old lady on her way to church, I picked out a route down the huge slope and committed, Rodney followed. Without a front brake all I could do was trail the back one softly so as to not go into a sideways slide. The bike kept picking up speed but I was in control, the warm golden shafts of the sun hitting me straight in the eyes; I still knew where I was headed but couldn't really see any detail on the track, made it through some tight switchbacks and was on the home straight when physics interrupted me again; this time the motorbike's front wheel slotting into a deep crossways rut in the road which snapped it sideways and brought the bike from 50 kilometers an hour to zero in the space of a few centimeters.

Another strange sensation, I thought how bizarre, how bizarre, two in one day; then the bike stood upright on its front wheel before launching into the air like a springing panther. The view from up there was good, I was an impressive 15 feet above the track falling steeply away from me and again this peaceful sailing feeling, wind in my hair, the bike pancaked onto its right-hand side and then we rushed groundward and the thought flashed through my mind: this one's gonna hurt.

The bike, me, all landed on my right knee, my head came down sideways and hit the handlebars or maybe the broken clutch lever, we bounced up again and the bike righted itself so that on the next landing, a little softer, I nearly castrated myself on the petrol tank and this time my chin smashed into the handlebars' gooseneck, one more small bounce then again the inevitable sliding, sliding, please stop sliding, get this fucking motorbike off me, is that my leg burning on the exhaust? Smells like pork, what am I going to do about my passport, I need my passport. No, just focus on crashing; fuck your fucking passport. Oh shit! This fucking kills already, until finally somewhere close to the bottom I ground to a stop and wrestled that fucking lucky color best brand yellow not blue motorcycle off of me. Fuck you.

I was nearly knocked unconscious from that dog shot to the chin but I knew this was no time to be passing out. I gathered my right leg up and took a look at my knee. What the fuck? It was as though someone had used a cookie cutter to neatly remove the skin, flesh and kneecap; I was looking at a perfect circle, thinking how odd, I'm not supposed to be able to see what my knee bone looks like, when the walls, fleshy pink and white and dotted with little capillaries, first oozed then gushed blood and the odd little universe I'd been peering into became a lake of thick, red soup.

'Fuuuuuuck!'

Rodney pulled up (actually he sort of fell), dropping his bike and stumbling to where I sat and looked at me, gaping.

'Fucking hell, look at my fucking knee. This is seriously fucked up.'

'China, have you seen your fucking head? Fuck your knee.'

'What?'

'Turn it to the left a bit.'

I rotated my head, noticing a warm, sticky feeling running down my neck and over my chest, as Rodney leaned in, said something like fuck and fainted, falling flat on his back. Fucking great. I dragged myself over and gave him a shake, slapped him a few times, perhaps a bit hard. Fuck it, nothing. Think, Piers. Hospital. The hospital's somewhere close to Thong Sala. Or is that Hat Salat? Whatever; it's north and it's over that fucking mountain and I need it bad. Fuck, can't ride over that mountain. No fucking way.

I managed to stand. Erratic, but I was up; the right leg appeared to be working. I looked down. The side of my torso glistened red. I bleed, I thought, I bleed red blood. My right calf had another thing going on, a rivulet ran down it, my left sandal was brown but the right one a nice burgundy. I took a step and it was sloshy and a bit slippery so I kicked the sandals off. Rodney started mumbling something but I didn't have time for that. The sun was setting fast, I scoped the area. There, one house several hundred meters down the track. Parked out the front; a four-wheel drive SUV pickup. Perfect. Taxi, and he's home.

I walked straight into the house, no time for civilities. It was basic, a lounge cum kitchen area and no-one in sight.

'Hello? Hello?'

'Hello,' it came from out the back, a man's voice. I walked through the kitchen and spotted the door to the rear balcony. Burst through it onto a timber deck, two young Thai men on a lounge, one of them in shorts and a blue singlet pulling on a bong. He looked up at me, coughed and said, fuck, as eerily white smoke circulated around him.

'I need to get to the fucking hospital.'

'Fuck, you no looking good. What happen?'

'What do you fucking reckon? Please, can you drive me to hospital?'

His eyes flickered half-closed.

'Awww, no way, too stoned. Cannot drive over mountain, sorry.'

'Fuck, fuck,' I was about to go into shock, I could feel waves of some sort of electric current coursing through my body. 'Water. Can you get me some water?'

'Water, sure, no problem,' he got up and went inside, came back with one of the one liter bottles of purified water they sell all over the island. I thanked him and skulled it all in about two seconds. It settled me straight away; good. Focus. I looked at the other guy; you could've blindfolded him with a piece of dental floss. Phuouc dat; I walked out of there and back to the motorbikes.

Rodney was sitting up. I told him I needed a ride to the hospital.

'Not feeling good, old boy. And don't think there's any way I'd be getting over that mountain in the dark, with or without you on the back.'

Fuck it. I picked up best brand Suzuki lucky color; the fucking trooper looked okay. My right leg had started shaking and I wondered about all that lost blood, I climbed on the bike and picked up my right leg which seemed to be some sort of inanimate attachment and positioned my foot on the peg. Suzy started first time, fucking A; I gunned her and stood up over the bars, smashed the gear lever down to first with my good foot and dumped the clutch. Either out of sheer determination or desperation I made it straight up that fucker of a mountain, the back end twitched and wriggled and threw itself around like a fish out of water, but after a minute or so of pinning that motor in the powerband and juggling first and second gear I was back up the top. My vision was crowding in, this creepy, absolute darkness encroaching from the sides, the bike's dim headlight beam was all I could focus on and the whole setup got wobbly and I bit through my bottom lip to keep it all together. Blood in my mouth; oop-a that fucking hurt. Good. Pain is good, pain means you're alive, you're awake. Fifteen, maybe twenty minutes to go. Lucky color yellow not blue bore me through the doom ride and before long I was on paved roads, negotiating streets that were in some strange way suburbia: houses, cars, ooh a cat, there's a road sign. What the fuck does it say? Oh well looks good, let's go that way anyway.

Twenty minutes later I realized I'd been down this street before, that one too. Where the fuck was I? I banged a left; looked familiar, or was it? Ahead, a Thai man walking, hand out, middle finger extended. Hitch-hiker, cool. I pulled up.

'Hello. Oh shit, you okay?'

'Need to get to the hospital.'

'You know way?'

I looked at him and shook my head.

'Okay. You a mess and I wearing nice clothes, but I show you. I live same way,' he straddled the bike behind me, placing a hand on my shoulder. 'Go straight. Try not to bleed. '

'I'm trying.'

'Good, thank you, next to the right.'

We made our way through the tropical burbs, a network of winding streets and greenery with loosely spaced houses and driveways. The occasional street lamp bathed the surreal scene in beautiful golden light. Hang on, this isn't a moment of beauty. I could feel the blackness closing in again like a tunnel collapsing. Focus.

'Okay, goodbye, good luck,' he was standing on the side of the road and I was stopped.

'What, where's the hospital?'

'We go past, I show you. You no remember?'

'No.'

'Easy, go back two streets, left, then three streets, right, one more, left, then you see, no problem.'

'You're fucking kidding me.'

'No.'

I pulled away, called out goodbye.

'Try not to die.'

Okay. That was weird. The walls were crowding in and my right leg locked up so I had to hang it straight. Not even a back brake now, get to the fucking hospital.

I dropped the bike good brand lucky color yellow not blue in the driveway of the emergency department and whatever power had been keeping me together vaporized, everything instantly hurt, pulsed, throbbed and burned as I stormed into the triage room. It was empty bar two nurses.

'Help me.'

'Ohh, what happen with you?' one nurse caught hold of my elbows as I pitched forward, the other one jumped up to help; they guided me to a gurney and helped me onto it. Arrived and at rest after all that mind projecting and adrenalin, it really started to kick. My knee throbbed and felt numb at once with a dull ache emanating from the very middle of the bone and my whole leg convulsed. Something felt cold and exposed around my right temple, an angry pain, and my skin blazed all over. My breathing turned shallow and faster and the nurses tried to calm me, one had a hand on my head and the other, a younger one, ran her fingers over my chest in a soft, tickling motion. Mmm, that felt good.

'You smooth chest, sexy, like Thai man,' she gave me a little pinch. The other nurse cooed and joined her colleague stroking me. What's happening, this feels nice; no, no, what the fuck?

'Get me a fucking doctor.'

'Ohh so sorry, no doctor here.'

'Where the fuck is he? Can you call him?'

'Doctor not even on island, he come in the morning.'

'Fuck.' Think Piers, think. 'Morphine. Get me morphine.'

'No, no painkiller, you have head injury.'

'What, so?'

If concussion you cannot have painkiller, very dangerous. You must wait for doctor to check.'

'When, tomorrow?'

'Seven am.'

Fuck. One of the nurses went away and returned with a shiny metal bowl filled with warm water and disinfectant and started wiping blood off me. 'Ouch, you have cut all over.'

'You're saying ouch? You fucking try it. Get me morphine, please. Codeine, anything.' It was wasted on them; after they cleaned me up the young nurse asked me to sit up and the other left again, returning with huge horse syringe, at least 50 mill, and a basin of water.

'Saline, we need flush out dirt,' she filled the syringe, no needle on it, and forced a jet of water straight into the hole. I virtually shot up off the gurney. 'Stay still please.'

'Fuck.'

They repeated the exercise over and over and it wasn't feeling any better since the first time. The older nurse gave me a rolled-up hand towel to bite on and eventually they seemed satisfied and bandaged up the knee and a few other points. 'You have hole in head,' said the younger nurse. I asked for a mirror. Oop, that wasn't nice to look at; it was a small but deep gash with an inflamed triangle of skin right by my temple and something white at the bottom. The older nurse put some butterfly stitches over it, the younger one gave me a glass of water and they left, back to as they were an hour before. 'You wait now for doctor.'

A clock on the wall; it wasn't even 10 pm. Eight hours till the doc arrived, no fucking way. I got up and almost fell over, my right leg stiff as a flagpole and just as unfeeling.

'What you do?'

'I'm outta here. Thanks for the dressing.'

This time I killed the engine and dismounted at the top of the hill and with the bike in first and riding the clutch against the dead engine I had some form of brake as I walked the thing down that fucking hillside. An hour later I was back at Haad Rin. The chemist was closed. I banged on the door and went around the back anyway. Nope. In the main building by my bungalow I found Somboon watching a movie with about a dozen guests or blow-ins.

'Fuck, what happen, man?'

'Motorbike.'

'Ah, motorbike do that to everyone.'

'Hey, have you seen my friend Rodney?'

'Rodney?'

'He's tall, taller than me, with blue eyes and long dark hair but with bald patches all over, missing one eyebrow.'

He shrugged, 'I don't know, you guys all look the same to me.'

I gave him an unconvinced look.

'You do!'

'Can you get hashish?'

Somboon found me a grape-sized ball of charas, a soft and juicy kind of hash, and a chillum to smoke it. Back in my hut I drew the sticky, sweet vapor into my lungs and held it there. The stiffness and tension started to dissolve away and the pain ebbed. At last. Fuck that doctor; I sparked up another chillum. It was amazing, I could feel blood and some warm, buzzy energy flowing into the fucked-up areas, thinking so this is what this stuff's really for. Thank fuck for Somboon and Ko Pha Ngan's liberal stance on drugs.

As for Rodney, I never saw him on Ko Pha Ngan again, though he did try to contact me about six months later in Australia.

The next morning was as fun as hell on the hottest day of the year and I was hella concerned about the sensations and even more so the lack of sensations in my leg. Functionality-wise it was as though I had a piece of dead timber strapped to me but bristling with supersensitive nerves. The SUV taxis went over the mountain to Thong Sala ferry port periodically, but they crammed the rear bench seats with ten or more farangs all chipping in for the fee. My leg wouldn't bend and I needed the whole bench to myself. The driver negotiated a price; 250-baht return to the hospital.

The routine went on for days. The doctor had buckteeth and thick-lensed black-rimmed spectacles, a Thai Jerry Lewis, and every day one of the nurses scrubbed my knee wound with a stiff steel brush until it bled again. Ridiculously painful, apparently it let the wound build back up in layers so as not to leave a crater-like scar. 'We see all the time. Motorbike, many crashes.'

'Yes, yes, they do it to everyone.'

'Yes, everyone.'

After a week of excruciating lifts bouncing over the mountain and brutalizing my wound I'd had enough; my money was running low and I decided to take over my rehabilitation, staying down the south end at Haad Rin. I fashioned a walking stick from a tree branch, carving intricate details into it, with a leather-bound handle and amber and red coral inserts. I bought bandages and salves from the chemist and applied tea tree oil from my medical kit. The smaller injuries were healing well, my head had also closed up but had a large swollen lump, and it took an agonizing month of charas and adapted yoga positions to finally start to get some bend into my knee. Money was thin and I rang a friend back home who owed me $3000 and arranged for it to be wired over, and the bungalow owner, a nice old Thai man, totally flagged my rent, which had already been at a super-low long-term rate.

I walked a little further each day, scraping along at tortoise pace with a protracted, lilting limp. I went to see the motorbike man who told me the bike had cost 40,000 baht to repair.

'What? How much can you get a fucking new one for?'

'New one no good. This one best bike, Suzuki, best model of best bike, very good.' He hung onto my passport and I returned a few times until eventually we settled at 20,000 baht, around a thousand Australian dollars, to be paid when my new money arrived.

'I need my passport so I can pick up my money transfer from the bank.'

He still hung onto my passport anyway. On the way back, I passed boss dog's house. Boss dog was awesome. The island's dogs were a mixed-up mongrel soup, resulting in a generic wiry street cur, the odd dilution of beagle or dachshund changing it up here and there, but boss dog must've been brought over by some farang and left behind; he was a massive jet-black pit bull with muscles on his muscles and all over the island you could see sons and daughters of boss dog; half pit bull, half generic cur. Boss dog and I were on good terms and as usual, as I passed I admired him. This time, though, he became unsettled, growling, then he leaped at me and grabbed a mouthful of ankle, unfooting me so I fell onto my side.

A Thai barman from one of the clubs on the front strip came out of the house and got boss dog off my ankle and he slunk back to his porch, still growling. What the fuck was that?

'Sorry. You make him spooked.'

'What? I didn't do anything.'

'You must think like dog. You go past him slow, flow change like pacing, holding big stick and look him all the time in his eye. He think you stalking him so he attack first.'

Think like dog. Good advice, and made sense. Sun Tzu would approve.

I ran out of money. Nothing new, but now I couldn't eat. That evening there was a knock on my door and Somboon was there with a kettle and two polystyrene cups of Mama Noodles. He left the kettle behind and the next night came back with two more cups of noodles. I don't know how he knew that I couldn't afford to eat, it was a touching gesture and I looked forward every evening to our meal together.

The wounds were all closed, the lump on my head had eventually ruptured and about half a liter of thick pus came out, but now my knee was swollen like a grapefruit and my ankle and lymph node in my groin were also inflamed. It wasn't looking good and I convinced my old taxi driver to give me a lift back to the hospital. Jerry Lewis was in, he saw no problem.

'We cut all open, clean out start again.'

I didn't have insurance and definitely baulked at the thought of going under the knife in an under-resourced hospital outpost on a tropical island, 12 hours from Bangkok with first rate hospitals and easy access to a plane trip home.

'Really, you want to operate?'

'Yes, we start again, no problem.'

No problem; I got the fuck out of there and never went back.

A day later I decided to walk to the other side of the island, Haad Rin Nok. The island was so narrow at this point that it was usually only a 15-minute walk. The pathway ran as straight as an angel's flightpath through a level grass field and coming the other way, scraping along on his walking stick, I saw Tepsi in the distance. Tepsi was 98 and looked every bit of it, posture like a cashew nut and with deeply wrinkled skin like brown not green Yoda. Ten minutes later I could make out the color of his hat, five more and I could see the whites of his eyes. Onward we pressed, until no more than 20 minutes after I first spotted him I could hear his walking stick prodding into the sandy pathway and his bony bare feet shuffling along. We both arced out to give a small berth and drew abreast.

He gave me an almost imperceptible nod.

'Sawadee khap.'

'Sawadee khap.'

Those awkward few moments when you don't know what else to say or do, then we slowly drew away.

The swelling halved again and I could bend it a tad or two, but my knee was uber-munted and not improving at anything like the rate I'd hoped for. It hurt just to take a step and was weak in any direction with virtually no lateral stability nearly two months after my accident. I'd planned to stay down south for four months but was trying to prepare myself for the disappointment of an early return home. My $3000 lifeline had arrived and I was eating well again, having returned Somboon's kettle and ingested enough Mama Noodles for a generation of rebirths and two-dozen reincarnations. Somboon and I celebrated with dinner followed by a big night, on me. The following day is not one of my most cherished, but was memorable nonetheless.

One morning I was woken early by rapid knocking at my door. I opened it to see a young Thai guy I didn't recall seeing before standing down on the grass; no shirt and sliced and diced like a body builder crossed with a rock climber.

'Hey, I watch you for months, you do good. Now is time for training,' he beckoned and I grabbed my stick and followed. As we ambled along he told me his name was Archie and he was a Muay Thai fighter. No wonder he looked like that.

'I get same injury as you in the ring, cannot bend knee for long time.' He snapped out a high kick followed by a knee rush. 'Now, 100 per cent.'

Archie led me to some thickets of bamboo down by a spring. 'We get the young piece like this one, see?' he pulled it back and let go, it whipped away. Then he struck it with his shin, soft roundhouse kicks over and over. 'It bend easy and also give little push back. Very good for knee, you try.'

I kicked a stalk of bamboo about the same size as his, it was perfect. No jarring, I could feel it working the muscles but without any pain. We kicked away for about ten minutes then he called the session over.

'Tomorrow morning I come for you again. We go 15 minutes, keep build up each day, okay?'

'Wow, thank you.'

'No problem. Seven o'clock, be ready.'

Archie was there seven days a week at 7 am on the nose. True to his word we built the training sessions up until he was spending a full hour with me every morning. Afterwards I'd invite him to breakfast or tea at the restaurant but he never accepted.

'See you tomorrow, champ. Seven o'clock, be ready.'

After a few weeks of training my knee felt strong and I could fold my leg in two, I was ecstatic. One morning as Archie arrived I walked down my stairs and towards him without my stick. His face lit up and he high-fived me.

'I'm fixed, all good.'

'No, training just begin.' That week Archie had me hopping on my right leg until it gave way, the next few days he made me lie beside a bamboo stalk and flex my ankle, extending and retracting my foot to rock the bamboo back and forth. Once I mastered that he cut off a length of bamboo and bound an end to each of my feet with twine and I'd lie on my back and pretend I was riding a pushbike, then finally he hobbled me with a whippy young piece of bamboo, affixing it around my ankle, knee and upper thigh.

'No training tomorrow, you wear for three days, I come back to see you.'

The bamboo brace made it hard to walk and I had to learn to push through it, but again it was a jar-free high resistance device and never made my knee hurt. Three days later, about a month after he'd first knocked unannounced on my door, Archie came back and took off the brace.

'How you feel?'

'Fucking great, look at this,' I bounced around, leapt into the air then stood and bent my leg with my full weight on my right knee.

Archie smiled. 'Well done, you are finish, very good.'

I still couldn't convince Archie to join me for so much as a drink let alone a meal, thanking and praising his generosity and patience, when eventually he conceded maybe there was one thing I may be able to do for him.

'With pleasure.'

He led me inland to a collection of concrete bunkers with tin roofs in the deep vegetation, a manually operated well nearby and the mandatory satellite dish bolted to the roof. We passed an elderly lady in a cane rocking chair who smiled at us, and went into Archie's room. He fished around in his cupboard and returned, presenting me with a weighty silver medal about as big as a saucer threaded onto a wide black and silver striped ribbon.

'I win this in Amsterdam, Muay Thai.' He pointed at an inscription. 'What is it saying?'

'It's Latin, I learned some in school,' I took a look, frowning. '*Autibus teneo lupum*. It says, um, hold the wolf by its ears.'

'By its ears?'

'Yup.'

He scratched at his ear. 'What does this mean?'

'I have no idea.'

'Hold the wolf by the ears. Okay, thank you.'

Clear as mud; I wished I could've helped him more. I returned to my bungalow and lay down, appreciating just how beautiful and selfless the generous spirit of the locals had shown itself to be in this strange and wondrous place. From minute gestures to gigantic; I could never have made it through without them.

The following evening, I showed up for work to kick off the evening's entertainment, dancing the crowd to its feet with the Monster Mix of 'Insomnia'. I was still a bit stiff myself and it'd be some while before I could once again crank it at my earlier level but the crew were all delighted to see me, and the Singhas ran fast and tasted beyond delicious.

Thailand. Like anywhere shit happens, no doubt crazy sh*t every day. But crazy sh*t is neither good nor bad it just is, and as well as dishing it out, sometimes Thailand has this unforeseen way of sorting it back out again, and that's one of the reasons I always hunger to return.

Several years later during my next stay on Ko Pha Ngan I crashed a motor scooter on the blacktop and got to see the insides of my other knee as well.

But that's a different story.

CHAPTER 11

BONKERS IN HONKERS

Simon Williams

The Hong Kong policeman decked out in his impeccable pressed uniform is incredibly polite, or perhaps he is intimidated by me. I stand a good foot taller, weigh 30 kilos more and my blood alcohol level is leaving his in the dust. The thin bath robe I am wearing starts to cling to my body with the soaking I receive in the tropical downpour. Underneath the flimsy terry toweling I have nothing on. Traffic is steadily backing up in all four directions of the intersection we are standing in the middle of. I can't see what the names of the streets are, all I know is that I am miles from my hotel, when the cab ride from Hong Kong Stadium to my lodging should have been less than five minutes. Just because I knocked back 10 or 12 beers more than I should have, the taxi driver thought he could pad the fare by taking me on the scenic route. Bloody cabbies.

This is the first time I have ever engaged in a heated argument with a cab driver over a trumped-up fare. Well, if I don't consider that one time in New Delhi, or that little thing in Cape Town, or the few times in Brisbane. But never had the police become involved. Well, except for the occasion in New Delhi. Certainly, this is my first incident in a financial hub of South-East Asia and an unprecedented first while dressed in bath wear.

I've never been a big fan of taxi drivers, I don't know many people who are. On my list of people I don't care much for, they sit below Seventh-day Adventists, telemarketers and drug smugglers. That means someone like Schapelle Corby rates higher than the average yellow cab operator in my book. If you drive a taxi and want to raise your class standing in life, go smuggle pot into Bali. Why this animosity towards cabbies? Because when I sit down in the back of a cab with a skin full of piss, they all try and take advantage of me. On one occasion in Brisbane, a taxi driver who only had to drive on a straight shot down Coronation Drive to get me home decided he wanted to pass by the base of Mount Cootha, which is 5 kilometers and two suburbs off the beaten track. So, within the context of my historical loathing of taxi drivers, it was clearly in the Hong Kong driver's best interest to take me straight to the hotel and not meander through every side street and back alley he could find to increase the fare.

Hong Kong is a schizophrenic-paced city and nothing gets the locals more out of whack than a drunk gringo prancing around a busy inner-city juncture wearing an item of clothing reserved for attire in an average bathroom or Hugh Hefner's wedding. But my motto when traveling has always been, when in Rome don't do what the Romans do – they pissed away their entire empire. This is one of those precarious moments while traveling abroad when it is necessary to go full dickhead.

This is why I normally travel alone, or perhaps why no-one wants to travel with me. I haven't worked out which yet. Only when on a rugby tour, am I tightly ensconced with a group. Unless the entire squad loses me, and this occasion in Hong Kong is the first time that has ever occurred. Well, if I don't consider that one time in England. Or the time in South Africa after that taxi incident. But they were both one-off anomalies. Not at all like the time when I was abandoned in a New York City hospital while the team went out drinking.

Full dickhead is an ethereal state of being, where one empties their mind of rational thought and behaves in a manner of such opposed nature to the conventions of society that both citizens and law enforcement realize it is in their best interests to just let you go on your way. It is a manifestation of the fight or flight physiological state of hyper-arousal, often aided by copious amounts of alcohol, that renders a body unable to distinguish whether it is fighting or flighting. So, it simultaneously attempts to do both. This inner emotional turmoil renders the casualty a livid, villainous mess, but even the most vengeful antagonist is stricken with admiration at this condition. It has an almost charming bravado to it. I have used this technique to overcome visa issues, flight cancellations and unhelpful immigration officials the world over. It earned Ben Kingsley a best supporting actor Oscar nomination for *Sexy Beast* in 2000.

Anyone who has traveled will have certainly witnessed other voyagers attempting to go full dickhead on occasions. People unhappy to follow security protocol, travelers annoyed at being pulled up for being over their weight allowance for baggage, late arrivals frantically needing to explain they must jump the queue to make their flight. Often times their efforts to reach the state of full enlightenment fall short and they reach the level of illumination known as just a dickhead.

Screaming at the top of my lungs at a taxi driver parked mid-way through an intersection, while dressed in a night robe during a tropical deluge certainly elevated my level of consciousness to the higher state of being. What beating of a butterfly's wings on the other side of the Pacific led to this cyclonic outburst in Asia?

Three months previously I was sitting at a bar in Santa Monica, California vaguely organizing plans for a trip to Australia with my travel agent, teammate and close friend, Good Simon. Another teammate Corky was also at the bar with us. Out of nowhere, Good Simon states that I should get a stopover in Hong Kong, seeing as I am going to be passing close by when I head back home. I don't know where his inspiration to choose a layover in Hong Kong came from, with a plethora of direct flights available from LAX and any number of cities in South-East Asia falling under the umbrella of being 'close by'. It is an idea that I had not given a sliver of thought to prior to his drunken declaration.

'Maybe you could go to the sevens,' added Corky.

Being a rugby tragic, that sparked my interest even more. The Hong Kong Sevens is a near religious yearly event, akin to the Hindu pilgrimage to the River Ganges, without the need to bath in contaminated water infused with cow shit. It is the duty of every able-bodied rugby follower to travel there at least once in his lifetime to pay homage. The date of my planned trip to Australia coincided close enough to the event in Honkers that a cheap five-day stint in Bali could be worked in by Good Simon to make it seem possible for it all to come to fruition.

Then Corky gets back to me that an old colleague of his who had worked in Japan for several years played on a team that regularly competed in the Hong Kong tens, a less professional, but still highly competitive event, that is played over two days prior to the sevens. Two emails later and I have gone from merely establishing that Hong Kong lies within a circumferential radius of 7000 kilometers from Brisbane (and this qualifies it as being close), to being a reserve player on the Tokyo Gaijin touring squad – an assorted team of expats from Australia and England living and playing in Japan. Well, that escalated quickly.

Thus, my arrival in Hong Kong was not to be merely a spectator of this grand festival of sport, but to be a participant. The Tokyo Gaijin supply me with jersey, socks and shorts. One of my new teammates loans me a spare bathrobe to act as a samurai kimono, as our official team number ones. The squad is encouraged to go commando, in the time-honored Japanese tradition of men swinging swords around. Considering my unbridled thrill at partaking, it would have been a decent idea for me to remember to pack my rugby boots.

Thursday morning dawns. After a vigorous day on the playing field, the Tokyo side is rewarded with not only winning the plate competition but also the prize for the best dressed team of the tournament. The squad celebrates heavily at the post championship dinner and that is where an extra 10 or 12 beers may have been consumed by some members of the team. It is at this point of inebriation that splintering from a formed group is inevitable, and 15 white men dressed as samurai exit the banquet hall, under ominously threatening clouds, to forge their own paths back to the hotel.

I hail a taxi as soon as I make it to the curb, as the first pellets of rain start to plummet. Safely inside the cab, with the skies beating a thumping melody on the roof, I hand the driver a card with the hotel address on it. It had taken only 15 minutes to walk to the ground in the morning, so I am satisfied that the trip back will be short and sweet. I fall asleep.

I wake up with rain still pounding on the roof and the taxi meter clicking over to HK$400. This is US$50 for a trip of ten blocks and I am still not at my destination. That is why, with the taxi hesitating while halfway through an intersection, I leap out of the cab and go full dickhead. No-one is more surprised than the taxi driver, and to his credit he just sits there and doesn't say a word while I carry on ranting in the middle of the street.

The well-dressed policeman arrives and he receives a complete breakdown of the events leading up to this moment, starting with the beer Good Simon, Corky and I share at the bar in Santa Monica. I forget to mention that I neglected to pack my rugby boots, and I considered this a key element of the saga, so I backtracked through the story to make sure that I wasn't leaving any unexplained holes. His expression is one of bewilderment and shock, undoubtedly thinking how can this sane gentleman leave for a rugby tour and forget his boots? As is always the case, rather than deal with the criminality of the injustice that the driver has done to me, the policeman tells the taxi to leave the scene.

'What about me?' I ask.

'You can go,' the policeman courteously explains.

'No, I can't. You just made my cab leave. I'm screwed. This how you treat people in your city?' The policeman is even more bewildered; here I am chastising him for not arresting me and now trying to give him a lesson in civics. 'Listen mate, can you just give me a quick lift in the police car back to my hotel? I promise I'll have an early night.' The officer is almost in shock so he agrees to my request. The omnipresent power of going full dickhead is quite persuasive.

The police car pulls up outside the hotel and I find my way out of the back seat all by myself. Several of my teammates witness my arrival through the lobby window.

'How was your trip back?' I was questioned.

'Uneventful,' I reply.

Our departure on the Monday morning from the hotel is more organized. We have taxis ordered for a 10 am pick up to deliver us to the airport express train station in downtown. The taxis efficiently arrive 20 minutes early and we have the stragglers checked out of their rooms and squeezed into the cabs by 10.05. The motorcade arrives on time at the station and we unload our bags from the cars. An unexpected argument erupts, over the fact that the drivers want to charge us for the 20 minutes waiting they spent outside the hotel, because they were too eager for the designated pick-up time. The verbal exchanges are loud enough between the arguing parties that a squad of policemen soon turn up to adjudicate the matter. This is unparalleled; one weekend, two cab rides, six immaculately uniformed cops. Hong Kong has certainly put on a show.

I present myself to the Cathay Pacific counter and hand over my ticket to Bali and my passport. The polite lady behind the counter purses her lips as she peruses my travel document. It would appear I have a problem. My passport expires in four months and Indonesian law requires me to have at least six months left before expiration to gain entry to the country. Like two months is going to cause the earth to spin off its axis and crash into the sun. Who comes up with these inane rules? Politicians? The only group of people who can keep taxi drivers off the bottom of my list of most despised people. My flight to Australia isn't for five more days, I was looking forward to spending that time cheaply lying on Kuta beach and now some Byzantine law is going to prevent that.

'Isn't there anything you can do? I have paid for the flight to Bali,' I implore.

'You will be able to process a refund. You can stay in Hong Kong till your flight on Friday.' She offers.

I don't have the money or the desire to spend five more days in Hong Kong, especially with the attitude of the taxi drivers in this city. Considering the dire nature of my circumstances and weighing up all my options, I reach the only logical conclusion. I casually look around to make sure that airport security is at a comfortable distance, then go full dickhead.

The discomfort of the poor girl behind the check-in counter rises precipitously. She is at a loss as to know how to handle the situation. Airport staff don't get the same training policeman do. She frantically clatters her fingers over the keyboard and interrupts my performance with a nervous, 'I can exchange your flight for one to Phuket, if that is okay?'

'Sure,' I reply, 'seat by the window please and I'll be checking one bag.'

CHAPTER 12

HANDCYCLING TO LAOS

Warren Boggs

Laos is a wild, wonderful country and I have long wished to travel to this secret and mountainous land, which is one of the few remaining communist countries. So, I made a plan to visit. I would cycle from Nan in northern Thailand to Luang Prabang in the heart of northern Laos. What made this plan a little unique was the fact that I am a paraplegic and my bike is a handcycle – an arm-pedaled three-wheel bike with a full complement of 27 Shimano gears. I have planned this three-week ride so that I could celebrate the Buddhist New Year festival (known as 'Pi Mai') in the Laotian world-heritage-listed town of Luang Prabang.

1 April, Bangkok

Early evening in Bangkok and Mochit bus station is bustling on both departure floors. People sit in groups on chairs, on the floor, wherever they can, waiting for their ride. I join them with my unusual luggage (handcycle, tent and sports bag) and the ubiquitous can of coke. Travel and coke. This combination is a ritual I practice wherever I go, wherever I wait, wherever I have the chance to sit, observe and study a new place, a new culture.

Now I have time to overcome my guilt. You see, today I bought a VIP ticket to the town of Nan. I will travel overnight in comfort, if only I can justify to myself, my capitulation to such an indulgence. I thought that I did not deserve VIP travel. My best argument to negate my guilt so far is that since I plan to cycle over 700 kilometers through Thailand and Laos, I should be allowed the occasional travel luxury.

The bus station is modern and is air conditioned. However, the bathrooms maintain that old Thai tradition of four turnstiles and two no-nonsense ladies who make sure that people pay for the privilege of visiting the toilet. Whilst I have the three baht required for entry, my wheelchair cannot yet fly, so I am unable to get through the turnstiles and into the bathroom. No worries. I have an empty bottle and thus will wee. The two ladies were entertained as I pee as modestly as I can into my bottle next to them. One thing I quickly learnt about being a paraplegic is that I must be independent at all times as I cannot always rely on facilities being accessible.

My accidental punctuality has ensured that I have a four-hour wait for my bus. This serves me right for going VIP! A touch more guilt is further eroded with this thought. So far, so good – overcoming personal guilt is not an instantaneous process.

It's been quite a long while since I last embarked on such a journey. As I wait, I can't help but expect my old friend Bec to appear and pull up a seat next to me. My travel through remote and dusty places has so often been with her.

My thoughts keep returning to my baggage. Do I have everything? Tent, tools, passport, medicine and money? I remain in a state of blissful ignorance; the items I have forgotten remain forgotten.

The guys at my workplace in Bangkok all marveled at my handcycle and traveling gear this afternoon. A couple of people hopped on the bike and checked out all of its contraptions. Word soon spread as they discovered my bike computer, which showed a top speed of 57.7 kilometers per hour. The story spread fast – this is a very fast bike.

2 April – Into the noonday sun

The VIP bus proved to be an astute investment. The ten-hour overnight trip was wonderfully comfortable. On the bus I watch the morning sun rise over a plethora of craggy mountains. My spirits lift as I feel a sense of freedom sweep over me. My journey has started and I am a different man. My traveling character has been freed of its shackles and it feels great.

We arrive in the town of Nan early and I hit the northern road on my handcycle aiming to make it to the town of Tha Wang Pha. I ride with my wheelchair in tow, its front caster wheels kept off the ground. I scooted up the first few hills, expecting a joyous downhill run after reaching each summit. They never came. Uphill, flat stretch, uphill. I was soon all scooted out and then employed my other favorite riding technique, the Cliff Young shuffle. Cliff Young won the Sydney–Melbourne ultra-marathon by jogging at a walking pace. Now I ride at a walking pace. Phew! I am buggered!

I made a few interesting rest stops along the way and gave the traditional 'wai' greeting to kids on a number of occasions. The bike and my proposed journey were of tremendous interest to many people. Local curiosity and friendliness always make my coke and water breaks enlightening.

As midday approaches and after riding 40 kilometers, I pull over for a rest. The noonday sun saps all beneath it. The last 10 kilometers did indeed have a number of long downhill sections where I passed the 60 kilometers per hour mark on a couple of occasions (towing my wheelchair), but the uphill climbs have returned. I find myself near the banks of the scenic Nan River. However, this simply means that I am at the lowest point in the valley and that the only way onward is unfortunately upward. The mercury approaches 40°C. It is dry, hot and cloudless. I am exhausted, knackered and completely out of puff. I have drunk more than 3 liters of water and coke in the last three hours.

A pick-up stopped me some time earlier and offered me a lift. I declined, but still retain the driver's mobile number. Hopefully I will use it to go out to dinner with Mr Aye and his wife, Um this evening.

The sounds of insects, birds and the light road traffic permeate down the valley. Orchards, rubber and teak plantations seem to be the favored agricultural land uses in the valley. I sit and stare. My exhausted mind wanders aimlessly.

Three kilometers after my lunch break I realize that I cannot go on. It is not yet 2 pm, but I just don't have enough energy in me to make Tha Wang Pha. The hills and the sun have taken their toll. Towing 20 kilograms of wheelchair and luggage doesn't assist my hill climbs either. But I am now out of excuses. At the next village I will stop and stay for the night.

As I spy the next patch of roadside shade a short distance ahead, I look twice at the pick-up already making use of it. As I draw near, I can't believe my eyes. Sitting on the tailgate are Aye and Um, the two people who stopped to offer me a lift earlier. I can't believe my good fortune. After our first meeting a few hours ago, these guys remained concerned about my progress and came back to see how I was going. Well, well, well. Yippee. With relief I gladly accept their offer of a lift and am soon traveling the last leg in the coolness of their pick-up.

Um is a doctor in Pua, 10 kilometers north-east of Tha Wang Pha, while Aye works in Nan. We have dinner together in Nan but Aye and Um refuse my attempts at paying for dinner as an offer of thanks for their timely rescue. I stay on the couch at Um's house in Pua and feel energy return to my exhausted body. What a lovely couple.

I cycled 40 kilometers today.

3 April – Nan

I spent the day in Nan. Dinner was interesting. The whole family who ran the restaurant I ate at came and had their dinner with me. The food was great and their warm hospitality was welcome.

Tonight, the rains came. I was absolutely soaked upon arriving for dinner. And I loved it; wheeling in the heavy tropical rain, hands outstretched relishing nature's free spirit. At the restaurant I changed into a dry shirt and grabbed a beer.

Mr Aye comes around later in the evening and we go out for dinner, my second for the evening. As he drops me home, Aye tells me that Um has already paid for my room. Wow.

4 April – Mountain bus trip from Nan to Chiang Rai

I am out of bed at six and by seven o'clock I am on my handbike cycling from the guesthouse to the bus station. By 7.20 am I have my first punctured tyre. It is raining. I fix the puncture and arrive at Nan bus station at 8.15 am where I change into dry clothes. By 9.00 am I am on the bus to Chiang Rai. Phew! It's been quite a morning but things are still on track.

The bus traverses a rather mountainous route following numerous hairpin bends and endless climbs. The bus drops down to first gear frequently. What an awesome road. I make a small mental note – do not cycle this route! These uphills are something else!

5 and 6 April – Chiang Rai to Chiang Khong (Laotian border town on the Mekong River)

I cycle 50 kilometers over fairly flat country from Chiang Rai to Phaya Meng Rai where I spend the night. I lunched in Ban Mae Pao and hung out with some local lads. They made sure my glass was always topped up with Thai whiskey. I got stuck into a yummy noodle lunch. The boys paid for everything. Hospitality and immediate friendship in Thailand is absolutely incredible.

The next day (6 April) I wake up at 6 am and have started cycling on the road at 7:30 am. It is cool and overcast again. There is no sign of overnight rain. These are great riding conditions. My spirit rises. The road is largely flat over the first 35 kilometers. I follow a tributary of the Mekong for the length of today's 70-kilometer ride. The valley is dead flat and reasonably broad. On its western side, low and bumpy hills rise steeply. Their topography however has not curtailed the growing of crops on their slopes. Many of these slopes are bare and where vegetation does prevail it is just brush and bamboo. I see only the odd small tree.

On the valley's eastern side, a massive line of mountains looms above me. The overcast sky paints these giants in a hue of light blue. The cloud hides their peaks and gives the impression that these mountains are a great distance away. Their lonely foothills cower at their sheer size and abrupt ascent, rising 1000 meters above the valley.

I stop for a rest at 10.20 am after riding 35 kilometers this morning. The sun has now started to banish the cloud. I eat, drink and rest. I repair a tube punctured earlier this morning. I have cycled only four days so far and already I have had two punctures.

I rest for 1 hour and 20 minutes, but am unsure as to whether my body has been re-energized. I remain wary after my energy-sapping initiation on my first day out of Nan. I still have a further 30 to 35 kilometers to cycle today. The sun is now out in force and the temperature rises to the mid-30s. There is a slight breeze, however, and it is cool. I have so far experienced very little headwind on this trip. Good-O.

I am riding again and up ahead of me I see a motorbike with mum, dad and son pull over and stop. The young boy indicates for me to stop and as I do so, the father returns with a gift for me from a nearby shop – some bottles of cold water and yummy eats. It is another example of the generosity of the Thai and Laotian people.

At lunch I share a bottle of Thai whiskey with a local policeman before he excuses himself for police duty. I politely refuse his generous offers of a lift or a wife, but I did accept the Buddhist necklace he offered.

I arrive in Chiang Khong on the Mekong River late in the afternoon. I had a second puncture today 8 kilometers before Chiang Kong. After the day's 71-kilometer ride, I feel great and full of beans. I had no problems with the heat and sun today. To protect me from the sun I made sure that my clothes covered me from head to toe. The road was flat, but rough in many places. This slowed me down but did not sap my energy as hills would have.

I spend the night in a bamboo and straw A-frame hut close to the Mekong River.

I ponder where to go from here. Luang Prabang remains over 250 kilometers away and cycling there is not an option as the road is unsuitable. It is a dirt road in poor condition through mountainous country. I push such worries to the back of my mind and enjoy a Chang beer and quietly rejoice at the completion of the 125-kilometer two-day ride from Chiang Rai to Chiang Khong.

7 and 8 April – Slow boat from Chiang Khong to Luang Prabang
Over breakfast I meet Diego, a Chilean diplomat based in Bangkok. He tells me that he will be on the boat to Luang Prabang which leaves in about an hour's time. Tickets are still available and can be bought at this guesthouse. How easy is that? I buy my ticket and make my way to the riverside.

The slow boat to Luang Prabang is a journey lasting two days and 250 kilometers down the Mekong River. This is an amazing boat ride through wild and sparsely populated country. And I mean wild. There are no roads, no cars, and no towns for the entire journey. In fact, there was nothing in the landscape that even resembled a horizontal surface. This landscape is incredible. I live in Kalgoorlie-

Boulder, Western Australia, an outback landscape of big skies and open space. Here in Laos, endless mountains extinguish the horizon and crowd me in. This landscape is very strange to me as I am used to flat outback horizons and being able to see into forever.

For the entire journey down the Mekong River, the landscape was a picture of chaotic and steep hills. I soon came to realize why roads in Laos are such a rare commodity. The wild topography simply refuses the entry of roads to this landscape. The boat stops at the village of Pak Beng where we spend the night.

We pass a number of small isolated villages, none having more than 25 or so houses. What was refreshing to me was that none had any obvious signs of outside influence like TV, cars, motorbikes or electricity. The houses were all on stilts and made of wood with woven bamboo walls and grass roofs.

My fellow passengers for part of the journey included a large boar, a 4-foot Mekong catfish and a 2-foot carp. The presence of these characters gave rise to stories among fellow passengers of monster 7-foot-long catfish that dwell in the Mekong's muddy depths.

9 April – Luang Prabang

Luang Prabang is a very special place with a remarkable history. It has associations with royalty. The word 'Luang' actually means 'royal'. 'Bang' is the special bowl monks carry to collect their daily alms and 'Pra' is the respectful term of address given to people and items of high esteem in Buddhism.

Luang Prabang has been the base of national and religious power over times gone by. The town has real beauty and a sense of character. Now, since Laos opened its borders a few years ago,

Luang Prabang now also has western tourists. I sat on the street as the night market began to unfold in the tropical, mauve-colored twilight. I ordered a Laos beer, which came with a complimentary glass of Laos whiskey. Woo hoo!

In making plans for dinner I reflect on the fact that I just adore good hamburgers; burgers that are served on a large plate and are presented with a serious steak knife. One sign of a quality burger is that it is just too large to eat with your hands. Wowee! The cheeseburger I ordered turned out to be a GREAT burger. Heaven is a street market bar in Luang Prabang.

It cost A$5 for my burger, chunky fries, large beer (600 ml) and a whiskey. Now that's a bit of awright!

I ordered western food because, surprisingly, I found it is easier to find a western meal in this town than Laotian food. And after a year of not eating western food, I was looking forward to enjoying it again.

Later that night a strange and sudden sound awoke me in the middle of the night. Psssssssssss. It was an urgent sound emanating suddenly from the darkness next to my bed. As my waking mind slowly started to function, I realized that the loud hissing sound was obvious evidence of another puncture. This one however was in one of my wheelchair tyres and happened quite suddenly in the middle of the night while I was in bed!

The puncture tally grows. I have now had four flats on my bike, including one I fixed yesterday and now one on my wheelchair, which was obviously brought about by a puncture-inducing ghost roaming the midnight darkness. This is indeed unusual.

10 April – Luang Prabang

At 7.00 am I attend to fixing the flat tyre. Uh-oh. The leak is in the valve. This is a problem. I am not sure I can repair a damaged valve and I don't have a spare tube for my wheelchair (I only have spare 26-inch tubes for my bike, but not a 24-inch tube for my wheelchair). I am fortunate though because bikes are popular in Luang Prabang and I am able to buy a bike tube at a local shop and have it shortened by 2 inches to fit my 24-inch wheelchair rims. Perfect!

At dusk I watch the red sun set over the Mekong River. The twilight is still and calm. The Mekong flows silently by as the brilliant red fireball sinks gently below the hills on the west bank. Ethereal magic seems to appear in the tranquility and glow of this tropical dusk.

As I make my way down to Martin's Pub, flakes of super-light ash gently float over the town and over me. A hazy twilight smoke ambles down Phou Si hill. The red sun's magic was the result of a nearby bushfire. I witnessed a spectacular sunset and now, half an hour later, my eyes start to water and I inhale the smoke and the ash.

11 April – Luang Prabang

I have dinner at Martin's Pub. I am ill today and feel simply awful. I have a deep, throaty cough, an infected throat and enough snot to sink a battleship. No energy, no zest. I wait for my body to regain normalcy.

I am in bed by 7 pm.

12 April – My 33rd birthday in Luang Prabang

I am feeling significantly better, but am still a long way from feeling well. It's actually been four days of me feeling rather crook. I did go for a 16-kilometer handcycle ride up river today, but after returning I spent the entire afternoon in bed.

I enjoy a twilight dinner at Nao's Place. In celebration of my 33rd birthday today, I have ordered the bacon cheeseburger, a large beer (to start with) and a glass of whiskey Laos. Happy Birthday Waz!

I toast my absent friends. And I make a special 'cheers big ears' to Bec.

The best thing happened to me on the way over to Nao's Place. I got wet! I was splattered – twice! Pi Mai (New Year) is the water festival where water symbolizes the cleansing and renewal that is the Buddhist New Year. Whilst Pi Mai officially kicks off tomorrow (the April full moon), a few people have been out practicing today.

My first dousing occurred along the waterfront road. A blonde farang (foreigner) lured me close by offering a glass of beer. As I drank, however, he emptied a bucket of water down my back. Wicked! I am now part of the Pi Mai festival. The second soaking I received from a ten-year-old girl on the back of a motorbike who shot me with a water pistol as she passed by. A drive by shooting! Yippee. I now feel part of Laos.

At Nao's Place I watch the world go by and sure enough, even in this busy street market there is a farang out on his evening jog. Luang Prabang is a heritage town with an awesome and regal history but it is now in the mid stages of the fatal 'Khao San Road disease'

– the making of a universal homogeneous society. McDonald's and Starbucks will no doubt arrive here shortly. People living in the center of town will continue to disappear as rent prices spurred on by the burgeoning tourism industry continue their rapid rise, forcing people to leave. Whilst rapid development in Luang Prabang has brought paved roads and higher incomes for some, it comes at a cost for others – the homogeneity of society.

I am reminded of a Manic Street Preachers song line: 'The west scratches onto my skin, contagious like a suntan'. In Luang Prabang I witness but also represent the influence of the west embedding itself into an unprotected and naive society. It is unstoppable. The vast array of the world's cultures and languages fade from contemporary practice, overshadowed by the silent cloud of western cultural encroachment.

However, the western food on offer here is FANTASTIC. And so, I tuck in.

Nao's Place has now become known to me as 'Crazy Sheila Bar' after the fireworks of my birthday night. The local manageress went berserk around midnight and smashed half a dozen empty beer bottles, threatening the dozen or so customers with the broken bottle necks. She was ranting loudly in English about all kinds of stuff, but did not make any sense. I have no idea what provoked this woman into her crazy and violent behavior. All I know is that she was a little ticked off. Whilst ticked off people are commonly seen in Australia they are a very rare sight in Laos and in Thailand. I did manage to fight back by taking a couple of photos of the crazy gal after she smashed a bottle on the bar close to my head. The customers were very quiet and no provocation of the crazy lady was ever made by these customers. We simply sat in awe and watched. And after five or ten minutes of the ranting and bottle breaking we all left.

I got home very late with Steph, a girl I met at Nao's who was also celebrating her birthday (34th) at Nao's. She got lost on the way home so I offered her the spare bed in my room.

13 April – Luang Prabang

I spent all day in bed feeling the effects of last night, although I did spend an enjoyable lunch hour with Swain at Martin's Pub. Steph never left my room until 5 pm thanks to her killer hangover. I had a quiet dinner in town but was in bed by 7:30 pm.

14 – Luang Prabang

The weather is cool and clear. I had a late breakfast at Martin's Pub and hung out with Martin himself, a ten-month-old cutie who is the son of the owner. I observe very little Pi Mai water action so far this morning. The street is busy and school is closed.

The Pi Mai water cleansing comes out after breakfast. I have to join in. I spend two hours soaking every car, bike or motorcycle that comes past Martin's. Everybody gets targeted – handsomely uniformed policemen, monks, tough looking kids and well-dressed older women. What great fun. People ride by with their mobiles held up high and thus dry and receive a wetting below the shoulder. I witness respect and humility in this water celebration. No obnoxious behavior.

I rode 8 kilometers around town this afternoon and I changed from a Pi Mai predator to prey. I got drenched whilst on my handcycle. So many kids lined the road and poured water all over me and the handcycle as I rode by. Bags of flour and black charcoal powder were also popular in the splash-out. I love it!

However, I remain unwell and am in bed by 7 pm.

18 April – Last night in Luang Prabang

It's my last night in Luang Prabang. For dinner, I venture back to Nao's Place for a cheeseburger. There is no crazy woman, but by 7.30 pm the pub is closed. I had an enjoyable night hanging out with three Irish guys and a Kiwi couple I had met previously. It was a fun night. I also spent an hour at Martin's saying farewell to Swain and Martin.

Now I climb into bed and my thoughts turn to tomorrow's plan. I need to get up by 6 am at the latest to catch the bus to Vientiane. I have no alarm. I hope my body can act as its own alarm clock.

And it does do. Well, actually the roosters next door do it for me. The first rooster called at 3.37 am. I am up at 4 am and on the road in the darkness. I arrive at the bus station before 6 am.

Adios Luang Prabang. I am on the bus to Vientiane, the Laotian capital. The route is an incredible combination of massive mountains and wild rivers. And everywhere the land is tilled or burned, no matter how steep the slope. Many slopes were nothing but bare soil. A few crevices boast the dark green colors of the remnant tropical jungle. I see tall trees and deep, dark rainforest colors. Villages strung out along the contour, cling to the steep hillsides. Looking far below me, I can see the road we have taken. It lies directly below us, but some 500 vertical meters away.

I overnight in Vientiane and then on the following night I have a glorious bed on the train home to Bangkok. Thanks for an incredible journey, Laos.

CHAPTER 13

SHAKEN, NOT STIRRED, IN JAPAN

Emily Saunders

Japan is one active country. Previously I would have gone out on a limb and said it has the most seismic activity in the world, but actually Indonesia is more active than a toddler with ADHD after being given a can of coke for breakfast, and pips Japan at the post in the earthquake Olympics. Regardless, when the largest earthquake to hit Japan struck the east coast of Honshu on 11 March 2011 at 2.46 pm, I certainly wasn't measuring the statistics. Instead I was having the crap shaken out of me and wondering how I was going to get off the ancient rickety chairlift I was on, which was half way up the summit of a Japanese ski resort. I also certainly wasn't prepared for the carnage that was to follow; as myself, my partner and our two little children tried everything we could to get the hell out of the country in the days that followed – all while trapped in a snowy village in the mountains of northern Honshu with no internet, no phone reception, and no electricity or water.

I was no stranger to Japanese earthquakes, having lived there on and off for four years previously. I'd felt my first one at three o'clock in the morning on a freezing night in Sapporo, which shook me awake. At first, I had no idea what was going on, and awoke with a start to find all the cups in the cupboard smashing together while my 1960s apartment walls were making some really strange sounds – and this time it wasn't my elderly neighbors, crazy on sake and playing the Japanese drums at 2 am. I leaped out of bed and looked out the window, and saw that all the power lines were also shaking. As I put two and two together and debated whether to run outside or not, it all stopped just as it had started – suddenly and without warning. I went back to bed. I'd felt my first earthquake.

It wasn't the last. Sometimes I'd feel them during my English classes. I'd be realistically faking that I knew what a modal verb was, and suddenly the room would start moving. My students and I would all freeze and look at each other without making a sound, all of us clutching the sides of our desks, waiting for the shaking to stop. It always did. Nobody would really say anything, occasionally there'd be an expression like 'Aaoooohhhhh' (say it with a Japanese accent to make it more authentic), but everybody seemed to take it in their stride, and I did eventually as well. I'd sleep through big ones that came in the night, or keep reading my book in my Tokyo hotel room on the 54th floor as the giant building waved back and forth like a palm tree during a tropical storm. It fascinates me the way that they build those skyscrapers with huge metal rods in them, designed to sway. It's a strange feeling though, and mid sway you can't help but hope that the architects were completely confident in their choice of building design. So, while earthquakes didn't exactly terrify me, they of course made me pretty uneasy.

It was March 2011 and I hadn't lived in Japan for almost three years. I still liked going back for visits though, and in particular for the snowboarding. However, complicating our ski safaris were two little hangers-on that I like to call 'The Mini Fun Stoppers', although they are perhaps better known as my children. Eighteen-month-old twins and ripping it up on the slopes don't mix, strangely enough, and it was bloody hard to find a day-care center at any Japanese ski resorts that would take children less than three. I didn't trust myself riding with them strapped to my back. I could get down the mountain no problems, but I couldn't guarantee there wouldn't be several stacks and some general uncoordinated type of behavior that would see me buried in snow on top of my tiny offspring. So, we had to improvise. But never say never. After quite a bit of clicking, a Japanese day-care center at the snow was found at a tiny little 'locals only' mountain, one and a half hours from Sendai (by train) on the north-east side of Honshu, which is the largest and main island out of the four biggest islands of Japan. Japan is actually made up of 6852 islands, so let's not go into too much detail here.

Our Japanese trip had already kicked off on a high. My long-time partner had proposed to me on top of another Japanese mountain with an extinct volcano in the background. It would have been romantic stuff if I wasn't abusing him for making me hike up to the top of the summit in thick snow. We flew into Sendai, a city with a population of 1 million people, and because I had a friend who'd lived here for some time, I was interested in staying a couple of days and checking it out. I was overruled by my partner who was keen for us to get to the snow. I sometimes wonder what would have happened if I'd won that particular 'difference of opinion' discussion, as 24 hours later the airport we had landed in was completely flooded to the roof, aeroplanes were floating down the runways, the airport train station we waiting at was washed away, and the city I wanted to check out was partially destroyed. By the next afternoon the triple knock-out punch of earthquake, tsunami and nuclear meltdown saw entire towns washed away, massive damage to infrastructure, 15,894 deaths and 6, 52 people injured.

Tazawako, our destination, is located in Akita Prefecture and is famous for its large and deep lake, the deepest in Japan, so deep that it doesn't freeze in Northern Honshu's bitter winter. Tazawako's claim to fame is that a well-known and loved Korean soap opera, *Iris*, was filmed there. It turned out that the most famous love scene in the entire television series was filmed at the hotel where we were to be staying. The lovemaking room itself was set up like a shrine, and you could peer in from the doorway, but it was roped off, and there was strictly no entry. Upon arriving at Tazawako station we were picked up by the hotel minibus and whisked straight to our hotel. It was a funny little building, completely old school and extremely Japanese. I'm sure they rarely had foreign guests, and especially not a couple with a pair of blue-eyed little blonde twins. We were quite the celebrities, which was handy as our poor Japanese could only get us partially there. The place was a shithole to be sure, but it was a Japanese shithole and that is completely different from a Western shithole. Even though it was dated, uninspiring and shabby, and the decorations were ugly and the ceilings low, it was immaculately clean, the beds were comfortable, we had a bath, and everything worked. All the guests wore slippers and matching Japanese dressing gowns (yukata) around inside, which were provided by the hotel, and were accompanied by rolled belts, everything beautifully folded and stacked in a wooden box that lay at the foot of the bed. Dinner was cooked for us in the Japanese way, thus we were served several courses of excellent food (some of it, origins unknown) in the communal dining room come restaurant. There was a lot of smiling, a lot of bowing and a lot of expressions of 'kawaii' (cute) directed towards me. Or it could have been my daughters, I wasn't sure.

The next day we awoke to yet another dumping of snow. To say it was epic is pretentious and makes me sound like a 17-year-old male surfer scoping a break, but that's about the gist of it. Seven courses of breakfast later, I'd wrestled my kids into their padded ski onesies and we were on the hotel minibus and heading up to the slopes. It's useless to describe the outside scenery. All I could see was white. The first day at a new mountain ski resort is so exhilarating. You don't quite know what to expect, where to go or what to do. The air of anticipation makes you silent and contemplative as you take it all in behind the foggy windows of the heated bus.

The resort at the top was a tiny set up. It really was a local's mountain that doesn't even register on the Japanese snow tourism radar. There were cheap tickets, piss poor rental equipment, five-dollar meals and basic amenities. All the staff were geriatrics, and you just knew that the guy wiping the snow off your chairlift seat went back to being a radish farmer once the snow melted. Having a Japanese farmer help you onto your chairlift is so much better than having a hungover 20-year-old liftie called Jay, who actively resents you because he has to work and you don't and you're gonna get all the freshies man. Suck it up J-Dawg, it's called life buddy.

The childcare center was a tiny room, absolutely jam-packed with toys, there were no other kids, and the staff were two 70-year-old Japanese grannies who spoke not a word of English and almost lost their loads with joy when they saw our girls. My daughters couldn't speak yet, so the language barrier wasn't going to be an issue or anything. It was a win-win situation. They sure took a lot of photos of the kids, and we noticed that when we returned the following year, the ski resort pamphlets featured a lot of pictures of our daughters advertising the day care center. If there's one thing Japanese ad execs love, it's a foreigner promoting their wares. I once got a job doing an advertisement on television flogging a product called Vitaflux. Now it may sound like a powerful laxative, but it was actually a magnetic bracelet that was meant to stop your neck hurting. Strangely they dubbed the final version into Japanese, which sort of defeated the purpose in paying a Russian and an Australian to congratulate each other on their choice of therapeutic jewelry.

With the girls safely tucked away having an impromptu photo shoot and playing with an Anpan Man toy (a Japanese super hero made out of a sweet, bean-filled bread roll), we were free, free, freeeeeee! When you travel a lot with your children, organizing childcare is tricky. Without being able to coerce your parents into babysitting slavery, you often don't want to take your chance with randoms, because next thing you know, Marcella from the so-called reputable agency has pissed off with the kids and is trying her luck for a good price for them on eBay. So, when you finally pack the little buggers off successfully, the high that follows is intoxicating. Plus, we were at the snow! In a random resort deep in the mountains of Japan, coasting through a meter of fresh powder. Could life get any better?

The answer to that question unfortunately turned out to be a resounding no. After inhaling a giant bowl of steaming ramen noodles for lunch, we decided to spend the afternoon riding the slopes leading down from the summit. Now the summit chairlift wasn't like the other resort chairlifts. It was a two-seater, made from rickety wood, and it had no cover. It was basically a crappy wooden bench on a wire. It looked like the only original chairlift from 1920 or maybe even 1820, and sitting on it was brutal in the afternoon bad weather. But snowboarders needing their fix are suckers, and so it was up and down on the ancient 'chairlift of death', each snowboarding session down proving more exhilarating than the last.

Just after quarter to three in the afternoon we were on the lift and halfway back up to the summit when it came to an abrupt halt in the journey upwards, and started shaking uncontrollably. 'What is it?' said my partner. He thought perhaps the crappy old lift had broken. I knew what it was almost immediately, and hearing the people below me shout '*Jishin! Jishin!*' confirmed it. What I didn't know was how big it was. It definitely went for a lot longer than any earthquake I had felt before, and it was much more violent. We were shaking around like we were about to fall out of that bloody chairlift any second, and the metal pylons holding the chairlift wire up were waving back and forth all around us. It just wasn't stopping. That was the scariest part. It lasted approximately five minutes. We didn't realize it at the time but we had sat through a magnitude 9.1 – the largest earthquake ever to hit Japan and the fourth largest earthquake in recorded history, sitting it out on a tiny, shuddering wooden chair high up in the air on the summit of a mountain in the middle of nowhere during a snowstorm. It's estimated that this massive quake shortened the day about 1.8 microseconds, shifted the Earth's axis about 6.5 inches, and moved the country as much as 12 feet closer to North America. It also sent shockwaves into space. It sure was a big one.

The chairlift didn't start again once the shaking stopped. A few people down below were yelling up at us but our poor Japanese didn't allow us to communicate effectively as to what the hell to do. It was minus 15 and it was snowing hard, and all we could think about were our baby daughters. Were they okay, and how the hell were we going to get to them seeing as we were stuck high in the air with no way down. We considered jumping but it was much too high. So, we sat. And waited, and huddled together, absolutely freezing. Eventually the chairlift started up again. I learnt later that they managed to get a generator going and although it took five times longer than usual, we eventually reached the top. As we dismounted, another quake came. This was the first of hundreds of aftershocks we would feel over the next few days and it was pretty bloody freaky to feel one so close to the first. The thought 'avalanche' flashed into my mind for the first time and from then on it was a 'get me off this mountain as quick as possible' situation. We bolted from top to bottom as fast as we could, feeling yet another aftershock five minutes after the first. On the way down, we noticed that none of the other lifts were operating. All of the other occupants of the newer chairlifts were not so lucky as us. As their chairlifts never started up again, we witnessed some sort of complex rescue operation going on with a pulley system and people being levered down one by one.

We got to the bottom at last and entered the main building. It was in darkness and there appeared to be no power, but it didn't seem damaged. We heard people loudly shouting that a big tsunami was coming as they checked their phones in the last five minutes before the internet went down, not to come back on for another three days. We had one thing on our mind, but downstairs was empty. Our babies were not in the childcare room and all the people were gone. It was deserted. The man from the ski hire saw us and began to explain that he had helped the Granny childcarers outside with our little girls. He said they had thought the building would collapse so they were still outside in the snow. We went with him and were at last reunited with the girls. The relief was tremendous.

Everyone was standing around outside, and seemed slightly confused, but calm, and when the man from the hotel with the minibus turned up to collect us, we went with him without question and without collecting any of our snow gear. We didn't really understand how serious it was, and expected to be back at the mountain the next day.

When we got back to the hotel there was no electricity and the internet had gone down there as well. Our rooms were freezing and the water wasn't working either. To get drinking water the hotel staff were melting pots of snow on one tiny gas heater in the corridor. There was an ancient transistor radio with a very distorted reception. But due to our simplistic language skills, all we could get out of both radio and workers was that a big earthquake had come and a big tsunami not long after. We had absolutely no idea of the scale of death and destruction that was currently going on around us. And I do mean around us. If you could look at a map of Japan and see the damage and our location, we were almost completely surrounded.

That night the hotel prepared food for us – they served it in the only room in the whole hotel that had a fireplace – the previously completely blocked off 'Famous Korean Drama Love Scene Room'. Once only able to be viewed behind a rope, we were inside by the fire feasting on fish and our kids were literally bouncing all over the love scene bed itself. Good choice people, that was one cozy room. I was fairly gutted when we had to go back to our shitty freezing room and pretty terrified into the bargain. As I mentioned before, there were a lot of aftershocks. I was a bit worried about the building collapsing so I had a mattress over the top of the cot so the girls might have a bit more chance of survival. We all slept in our warm ski outfits and I had a bag packed at the end of the bed that I called my 'flee bag'. It contained money, our passports, a torch, some water, our shoes and various baby items. I had also worked out an escape route from the window. I hoped it wouldn't come to that. Outside the snow was meters deep and it was a balmy minus 25 overnight.

Over the next couple of days, the hotel began to fill up with people. We learnt that these people had been traveling in the vicinity by train when the earthquake occurred, and that all transport in and around the area had come to an abrupt halt. With nowhere to go, local hotels had taken in the train passengers. By this stage the hotel had really got their improvising down pat. Meals were now served back in the dining room. There were candles galore, and individual gas hot plates for each table. And the best part was that the kitchen was pulling out all their best goods from the deep freezer. So, while not far away people were freezing and trapped in cut-off towns with no supplies, we were eating lobster by candlelight. It's good I didn't properly know how bad it really was for all those people or I couldn't have swallowed it. Though it was pretty delicious, and waste not, want not…right?

It was during one of these elaborate dinners that after three long cold days, the power came back on. The whole room cheered and soon after we were back to our rooms to ring friends and family and turn on the television and check the internet.

I could not believe it. My eyes wouldn't process what I saw. The 40-meter-high waves laying waste to everything in their path. Those waves were so black and that water would have been so, so cold. It was hell, and all had been consumed – swallowed by the sea. Just like that, it took everything. It really was pure disbelief; the carnage, the fires, the bodies, the destruction. We had been sheltered from reality, in a kind of bubble. We had been fed and taken care of, with no real understanding of what hundreds of thousands of people were going through. It was confronting. What was the most terrifying for us was just how badly the situation with the destroyed Fukushima nuclear plant had escalated. Destroyed by the waves, it had reached crisis point. Nobody knew what was to come. Tokyo residents were advised to stay indoors because of the risk of radiation, all foreigners were trying to escape the country, and the roads to the airport were stagnant with massive amounts of traffic. Everyone wanted out.

Not sure what to do we just froze. Getting to Tokyo for a start would have meant a long journey by car, closer to Fukushima than we were now, with no guarantee we would be able to get tickets out of the country. However, we couldn't stay where we were either. The hotel was running out of supplies and they wanted us to move to a different hotel nearby. We decided that was not a good option. What about if the second hotel wanted us out after a couple of days? What about if the Fukushima plant completely destabilized? We became extremely uneasy. Of course, the airport we had flown into was not an option; we had seen footage of the tsunami pushing giant passenger planes along like they weighed nothing, and knew it had flooded to its roof. Incidentally, when we did fly into Sendai airport the next year, we could see how high the waves had been by the trees which were stripped of leaves and branches 10 meters up the trunks, and they all appeared bent and twisted by the force of the water. By chance, we found out that a small city in the far north-west of Honshu, Akita, about 250 kilometers away, had one international flight out of their tiny airport each week. This flight went to Seoul and it was happening early the very next morning. We had to get the hell out then and there. The hotel staff found us a retired taxi driver with a very old-school Japanese taxi who agreed to take us to Akita for a couple of hundred dollars. We went back to the ski mountain to get our gear, and insisted on being let into the main building to rescue our daughter's dolly she'd been bawling over for three days (apparently my partner emerging with a baby doll was highly amusing for all the Japanese staff who had initially resisted letting him back in the building).

I have no idea how we managed it, but somehow, we fitted the four of us, two snowboards, all our snow gear, three suitcases, a stroller and two travel cots into a tiny Toyota sedan – complete with those white doily things all over the seats that Japanese taxi drivers love so much. The hotel staff got teary when they waved us off, and sadly we never saw them again. The hotel had permanently closed by the time we went back there the following year. We had wanted to thank them for looking after us and making us feel safe, but we never got the chance.

It was strange being out in the world again. Although we didn't go near the damage, the characteristics of an apocalypse were all around us. Shops deserted, some boarded up. Not a single vehicle on the road, not a glance of another human being. For 200 kilometers we drove past the same deserted surroundings. The only time we knew that other people still existed was we passed by a rare open petrol station. Here we saw lines of cars and people all filling up containers with fuel. They looked like they were preparing for the worst. The country's infrastructure had completely shut down. Nothing was getting anywhere, especially around here.

At last we arrived in Akita. We were to spend the night, and we had found a room in a small business hotel attached to the train station. The hotel was called 'Alive'. We could look down into the train station as we passed by to get to our room. The whole train station floor was wall-to-wall people, all sleeping on flattened cardboard boxes with grey donation blankets on top of them. When all the trains stopped those people had nowhere to go. It had been days though, and I wondered at the time how many more days they'd be there for. After dropping off our bags we traveled into the town to try and buy milk for our daughters' bottles, some food and some water. It was like a ghost town. It was so quiet. And even where there were other people, nobody was talking, and there was none of the usual bustle, and laughter coming out from the bars and restaurants that lined the city streets, as they were all closed. It was impossible to buy anything as there was nothing in any shops – all goods cleared out except for 'diet bars', plus some crappy Japanese junk food, and a couple of boxes of grape juice. Even all vending machines we came across had nothing in them. No water. Thank goodness, we were leaving in the morning (touch wood), but what about everyone else? When would they manage to get goods in?

In the middle of the night one of our daughters vomited everywhere. The four of us were sleeping in one bed so it wasn't hard to get a good spray of chunks over us all. The poor little sweetie just couldn't handle the crappy processed food we'd fed her, and I'm sad to say that as soon as I'd cleaned up the sorry mess she technicolor-yawned all over the place again. It wasn't a great night's sleep, but it was never going to be – with or without the unexpected spew shower.

We were at the airport very early. There was no way we were missing that plane. It was completely full, with more people lined up outside the door taking their chance on getting any spare seats. The crew of the Sea Shepherd were there. They'd been making a documentary about Japanese whaling when the earthquake and tsunami occurred. In a couple of places, they were first on the scene to offer assistance and I think they'd seen traumas they'd never forget. One guy described seeing a woman just clinging to a bit of wreckage on top of the black churning water, being washed away and screaming and screaming, he was unable to do anything to help. Just watch.

After a long wait in the airport we were on that plane. I was feeling a lot of different emotions; obviously relief, but also like I was abandoning friends of mine still living there who I knew were also frightened. At the same time, I knew it was right for me, as a foreign tourist, to get the hell out of there so that the Japanese people could look after their own.

But it wasn't until we touched down on the runway in South Korea that at last, after four days, I actually cried. I cried my eyes out. For the tragedy and the loss of lives, for the trauma for a country that I loved and felt connected to. For the helplessness that you feel when something so far beyond your control occurs, for the gratitude for my children, and for my partner who got us out to safety. And I didn't stop crying for the next two days. I cried when I woke up, I cried when I walked around the busy streets of Seoul where life was going on like nothing ever happened, and most of all I cried when I watched the news. And when all the channels were saying that the Fukushima meltdown had the potential to blow Asia off the map, we knew we had to get further away. Japanese engineers couldn't initially stop the leakage at Fukushima. It took months to reduce the emissions. Radiation was found in local milk and vegetables, and even in Tokyo's drinking water, although briefly. It continued to leak into the Pacific Ocean, raising levels to 4000 times the legal limit.

We went back a year later – to the same place, tiny Tazawako. Flying into Sendai the damage was still apparent 12 months later.

And although we never got the chance to thank the hotel staff for caring for us and helping us get out of there, we did see the Japanese granny daycare workers who were beyond happy to see us (well maybe our daughters!) and other workers from the ski resort who recognized us from 'Tsunami Day' (as they called it). It was a strange feeling to return to that rickety old chairlift and ride it again to the summit, but I can't deny that despite the language difficulties there was a sense of solidarity in being back there. We had all experienced this intense event at the same time in the same place, and that meant something. They estimate the full recovery will take a decade, with areas affected by the nuclear disaster to take even longer to recover. Those who lost people they loved to the wave have a lifetime of sadness to carry with them.

But despite all of this reflection on the fragility of life, it still goes on, doesn't it? People rebuild their world and find a way of living with the emotional and psychological damage they've suffered. That's the utter brilliance of the human race; survival and continuity over devastation and despair.

To this day, 2562 people are still missing, and the Fukushima reactors are still leaking radioactive waste. Cleaning up the plant is expected to take 30 to 40 years. And despite shutting down all nuclear plants following Fukushima, the present government wants to restart the nuclear energy program in Japan again. Now that's crazy sh*t.

CHAPTER 14

THE INDIAN HOSPITALITY

Megan Jennaway

Our friend looked very different from the humble, pyjama-clad houseboy we'd met at the Hotel Kwality, Amritsar. Waiting for us outside the tea house was a small, skinny man in a brown polyester suit. His lopsided lump of black curls was unraveling in the breeze and his too-short flares flapped noisily around his ankles, as though he were about to set sail.

Mustana nodded at us briskly, indicating we should follow him inside.

'Hello,' we said. He did not return the greeting. A knot of disquiet was forming in my gut. Looking around at the panoramic mountain setting quickly soothed me. The village of Baijnath teetered on a flank of the Western Himalayas, hemmed in by a palisade of soaring white crags. It was stunningly beautiful, but appearances can be deceptive.

Mustana was not the only one waiting to greet us. At 6 am the sun had not yet climbed over the mountains, but already the chai shop was full of men, all craning their necks to observe our coming.

The two young boys minding the shop were sweating profusely. Neither looked more than ten years old. The shorter one had a woolen muffler wrapped around his head but no gloves. He kept tucking his hands into his armpits for warmth. The other boy was making chai. A large, soot-blackened kettle on the stove hissed and spluttered as he flung tea leaves into the water. As he added handfuls of sugar, cardamom pods, nutmeg and smashed ginger it almost boiled over.

As soiled cups piled up on the counter the boy dunked them in a bucket of water. I looked down uneasily into the turbid brown fluid. The cups came out not much cleaner and probably more contagion-ridden than when they went in, but they were earthenware, so perhaps this didn't count. I watched the boy's fluid movements as he whisked the cups through space, dunking them down then flipping them upright. A spiral of sweat flew off his face as he reached behind him for a metal beaker. Tipping it sideways he sloshed some milk into the kettle. It frothed up violently. Just before it boiled over he staunched the flame. Raising the kettle high, he poured a fragrant stream of chai into each cup, without spilling a drop.

Meanwhile our erstwhile houseboy, the chowkidar we knew as Mustana, was marching around the chai shop with his chest puffed out and his arms swinging. We trailed behind apprehensively. The patrons seemed to be expecting us. They nodded at him as he strode past, returning his wave. I felt distinctly uncomfortable. The men in the chai shop weren't looking at my face; they seemed to be deducing my gender from my lower anatomy. Either there were no women living here or they didn't drink chai in public.

'Let's get out of here,' I whispered to Dave. He too was feeling conspicuous. We headed for the door.

'Where are you going?' Startled by the harsh tone, we turned around. Mustana was a softly-spoken fellow, but it was he who'd called out. 'Sit down here!' he ordered, pointing at a table. 'I am bringing you the chai.'

The table was fully occupied, eight or nine men to a bench and some sitting on other's laps. Feigning incomprehension, I turned back and kept heading out the door. Outside the shop, the clientele had overflowed onto the footpath. Wrapped in blankets and turbans, men of various ages squatted on the ground. Some were gnarled and toothless, others dark-eyed and swarthy. All were huddled over glasses of sweet, milk tea, fragrant with cardamom. Inhaling deeply, we could almost taste the warm, reviving syrup on our tongues. Dave went back inside to order.

'No, no! I am giving you the tea! You are having the Indian hospitality!' ranted Mustana. I could hear him from the footpath. I wondered why he was suddenly calling it tea when even we referred to the national drink as chai. I watched as he elbowed Dave out of the way, waggling his head from side to side. Dave came back outside to join me. We watched though the window as Mustana called out his order and sat back down, a Big Man among his friends, laughing and joking as he poured whisky into their chai glasses and plied them with cigarettes.

It struck me that our chowkidar looked out of place in his ill-fitting suit and lace-up shoes. The men were all wearing the kind of clothing he'd worn down in Amritsar: thick woolen kurta-pyjamas under warm yak-wool or plaid coats, leather sandals and turbans wound thickly around their heads. Puffing on the their thin, hand-rolled bidis, they looked at him thoughtfully, accepting his gifts and glancing up at us from time to time.

I wondered what he was telling them. All he knew about us was that we were students, from Australia. And that we were married, a useful fiction we'd been employing since leaving Athens.

Our chai was taking a long time. Perhaps they'd run out of black leaf, or sugar, or maybe someone was milking the cows. Either way, nothing was happening. The kettle had disappeared and the kerosene burner had gone out.

Mustana appeared in the doorway. 'We are going now. Bus is waiting.'

'Wow,' muttered Dave. 'So much for the Indian hospitality.'

As Mustana latched on to Dave's sleeve I sent him a sympathetic look. They shuffled towards the waiting bus like shackled prisoners. Like a good Indian wife, I followed.

II

We'd been on the road for nine and a half months, making our way back to Australia from London. Along the way we'd been gypped by an unscrupulous branch of Magic Bus – Albayrak Tours – who'd dumped us in Tehran instead of New Delhi; we'd been arrested on the train from Peshawar to Lahore for harboring a pocket knife, the blade of which was longer than a (Pakistani) ten rupee note; and most recently we'd been set up for a drug bust in the Ringo Bells hotel, in downtown Lahore. Between us we'd suffered 14 episodes of diarrhea, 3 episodes of amoebic dysentery, and lost a lot of weight. With five more months of traveling left, we'd be thinner still before we got fatter.

I was not in my comfort zone, crushed up against the window. Mustana's village was a three-hour bus ride from Baijnath. I was already sleep deprived and now I was having caffeine withdrawals as well. Somehow our host had interposed himself between Dave and me, on a seat designed for two. His fruity body odor poisoned what little air was available. I gripped the chrome seat rails for balance until my hand was almost amputated as the loose seat-back snapped shut around a bend. The engine was in a commensurate state of disrepair: crunching into bottom gear for the steep ascents, sliding into neutral for the downhill sections and refusing to go back in. Like a runaway felon it loped away down the precipitous descents, while Mustana explained to Dave that the practice saved on fuel.

I was already quaking in my boots when suddenly, out of nowhere, a mass of glistening white rock loomed into view, blocking out the sky.

I'd never seen mountains until that moment. Everything else was just pretending.

III

After our harrowing experiences of Pakistan, India was bliss. We fell into the relative comforts of the Kwality Hotel like defeated cormorants, unable to complete our migration. The sheets were clean, no drugs lurked under the mattress or inside the drawers – for which we could later be busted – and the restaurant served scrambled eggs on toast, just like our mothers had made it. India was an English-speaking country, a member of the

Commonwealth, and there were gum trees everywhere. It was home, with an exotic twist.

Mustana struck us as a deferential, self-effacing little fellow, anxious to make our stay as pleasant as possible. Wearing nothing but a white dhoti with a ragged woolen jumper over the top, he plumped up our pillows, brought us steaming trays of chai, and listened in horror to our tales of woe. He was disgusted by the actions of those deceitful Pakistanis. 'They are all being thieves and rogues,' he said. 'Why are you not coming to my house? I am having a velly big family. Come and be seeing what is the real India.'

The real India. He'd pressed a button. Two weeks and several hundred kilometers later we rose from our beds at the crack of dawn and said goodbye to the enchanting Tibetan village of McLeod Ganj, where we'd been so happy. Harnessing our backpacks, we hiked the three kilometers downhill to Lower Dharamsala and caught a bus to Baijnath. From there, Mustana would escort us to his home.

If we'd known what we were in for that cool spring morning, we'd have turned over and gone straight back to sleep. But we weren't to know, and the real India beckoned.

IV

The man who'd become Mr K S Mustana – 'You can be calling me K S for short, isn't it?' – could not stop talking. Loudly. It was necessary that the entire busload of sari-clad peasant women and bidi-smoking laborers and ancient, bearded elders heard him. Only the feral children who clambered over people's shoulders and laps to ask for lollies, or vomit out the window, managed to ignore him. Leaving Baijnath, he elbowed us both in the ribs, pointing out a Hindu temple. 'Please be observing this temple,' he said, 'It was built in a single day by five brothers.'

'Really?' We stared out the window at the moss-covered edifice as though it might somehow authenticate the tale. But the temple was immutable, refusing to give up its secrets.

K S was not satisfied with our response. We'd missed the point, the one he was about to reveal to us.

'What you must be knowing,' he said, 'is that these five brothers are all being married to the same woman! They are all sharing her, isn't it? Sharing this same wife!'

Honking with delight he slapped his thigh, looking around at the other passengers to see if they'd caught on.

The journey continued. With K S exuding foul odors beside me and talking at the top of his voice, I could feel a headache coming on. Dave badly needed a cigarette but couldn't reach his bag. Gritting our teeth, we steeled ourselves for the journey. Three hours was not that long.

The road flicked like a serpent between rising bluffs, each steeper than the last. From time to time it flattened itself against a steep hillside, tipping the bus sideways. Other vehicles passed us on narrow mountain passes; oncoming buses had to reverse back to wider sections or cling to the edge as we inched past. More than once we were caught against unfenced escarpments dropping hundreds of meters into a river gorge. Indifferent to jeopardy, our fellow passengers erupted into coughing and groaning, sneezing and spitting. Some of the ancients voided bowels and bladders or spewed into handkerchiefs and folded them up again, as though secreting a precious jewel.

My headache worsened. The bus stank of shit and urine and bile. Dave had gone a horrible shade of green and I was only just holding back my own emetic impulses. Closing my eyes, I tried to pretend I was somewhere else. Then a child's dark-eyed face appeared above the seat in front and vomited across my knees.

After what seemed more like 12 hours than 3, I glimpsed terraced green fields amid tall deodar forests. 'We are to be shortly arriving,' announced K S. I felt myself relax. Soon we would arrive at Mustana's. There would be somewhere to wash. I could pull out a change of clothes from my pack, brush my teeth and hair. There might even be some of the piping hot chai we'd missed out on 12 hours ago. Or three. Restful eucalypts brushed past my window, making me nostalgic for home. Fantasizing about hot baths and clean sheets, Harris tea and toasted vegemite, I tried to catch Dave's eye. Immediately K S aka Mustana leaned forward and blocked my line of sight.

'You are seeing my land now, isn't it?' he shouted, above the din of the bus. 'I am having all this!' He gestured towards the window. 'This also! And this!' Pointing to the other side.

'Really?' Dave asked. 'It's all yours?'

'Yes! All of it!'

The arc of his wave encompassed everything we could see, the fields plunging downhill on the left side of the bus, the broad flat meadows on the right. Later, I would realize he was probably pointing out lands collectively owned by his family, his male kin – his father, father's brothers, their sons, his own brothers and so on. But at the time I didn't know how peasant societies worked. I assumed he was bluffing, Puss-in-Boots style. These were the lands of the Marquis de Carrabas.

The bus stopped abruptly amid eucalypt groves and verdant rice fields. No village in sight. Shouldering our packs, we wandered through the trees. Golden sunlight pooled around our feet. Iridescent dragonflies flashed among the foliage and hidden birds trilled in the breeze. I smiled at Dave, transported. He grinned back like a lunatic. What had we been worrying about? Mustana's village was heaven on earth.

On we floated, trailing after our host. Soon we came across a humble mud-brick bungalow, tucked beneath a neem tree.

'What a sweet house!'

'This is not,' said K S dismissing it with a wave. 'I am having a bigger house.'

Mustana the gentle chowkidar kept morphing into K S the jerk.

Another mud-brick bungalow appeared, then another, then several clustered together. We were coming into a village. Dotted everywhere among the trees were lime-washed pale blue or yellow cottages, set in small, neatly swept clearings. Crimson and red bougainvillea exploded beside fragrant white frangipani.

Mustana's village seemed a restful place, far from the madding crowds of the plains. I stole a glance at him. Sunlight gleamed in his hair and his gait seemed to have slowed. The humble chowkidar has returned, I thought fondly, my headache easing. Perhaps he was just tense earlier, due to the stress of bringing us here. Perhaps he, like us, was uncertain of how it would go.

The further we walked the fancier the houses. Tiled roofs replaced the thatch, mudbrick walls were rendered with cement and painted. Houses clumped together in the house yards like fungi, taller, larger. Upsized. I sensed an emerging class distinction: those on the outskirts being landless laborers whose labor paid for their rent, tenant farmers, who leased a plot of their own, further in, and those closest to the center owning most of the land, like Mustana's family.

We walked on.

It was dreamily quiet, eerily empty. Not a soul in sight.

Then the bubble burst. People suddenly appeared around us, populating the emptiness. Woodcutters, their axes suspended in space, stopped and stared. Farmers stood up from their labors in the rice fields and gazed across, eyes shaded. Leaning over the well, women froze at the sight of us, their buckets held aloft. Then movement returned as they all surged towards us. We shrank back helplessly. On all sides, villagers stared and gaped as though we'd just fallen from the sky. Everyone wanted to catch a glimpse of the strange, tall man with wild, stormy hair and the slender, dark-haired girl beside him. Their white skin was weird enough, but they were wearing jeans as well, even the girl. Especially the girl. The man was a mystery, hair like a sadhu but fully clothed. Skinny like a pauper. Tall like a freak. Perhaps he was a madman.

We shrank back. A rising babble of noise engulfed us. My headache returned with a vengeance. As the mob encroached Dave slipped behind me. His lunatic grin was gone and his ears twitched like a wallaby sensing danger. I looked to K S to whisk us away to safety but he was too far ahead to notice. As he disappeared into the crowd, I heard Dave whisper behind me, 'Wanna split?'

Split? Now? My head pounded with the urgency of making a

decision. Then K S turned and summoned us with a peremptory wave. 'Okay,' I said. But it was already too late: the villagers were clearing an avenue for us like God parting the Red Sea.

'You must be coming faster,' K S said. 'We are alighting now at my house.'

Easy as getting off a plane, I thought, as Dave poked me in the ribs, smirking.

Thank God, I thought. Almost there. I only had to steel myself through all the introductions, then tea and refreshments would be served and Mustana would kindly explain to them that I was unwell and needed somewhere quiet to lie down. I'd clean myself up, take a pill and Dave could keep me company while we both snatched a few hours' sleep.

Catching up to K S, I reminded him of my predicament. 'Sorry to be sick,' I said, confidentially. 'But I'll be fine after I've had a good rest.'

K S aka Mustana completely understood. 'Achha, achha, of course. There are plenty of beds in my house, no problem.' He promised that his wife would bring tea so that I could take a paracetamol. This was before the days of bottled water, and rummaging for the chlorine pills deep in my pack was beyond me at that point.

'Achha, achha,' Mustana repeated, rolling his head from side to side in a Spike Milligan nod.

'*Shukriya*, Mustana.' I beamed at him gratefully.

He led us to a shady clearing bordered with pink-tongued lilies and purple hydrangeas. Walnut and apricot trees broke up the light. Three lime-washed bungalows filled the house yard.

'Come,' said Mustana, stepping up onto the porch of the largest one. 'I am bringing you to my house,' he added, with a pompous tilt of his chin.

We stepped through the door into a large room. There was little furniture: a sofa with mirror-embroidered cushions, silk curtains billowing in the windows. Homespun blankets piled against a far wall. Neatly swept cow-dung floors.

Three women squatted with their backs to us beside a fireplace in the far corner. Over to the left, several opened onto the room.

I was looking at one when a young woman in faded cotton pyjamas stepped through it and almost screamed. Another followed and nearly dropped her armful of clothing. They stood there, gaping at us. A third woman stood up from the hearth and clapped her hand over her mouth. Seeing Dave, she pulled her yellow headscarf primly forward. Then a slender, middle-aged woman with a warm smile came over and took my hands in hers. She had a comb stuck in her unbound hair and smelled of sandalwood. Mustana has a lovely wife, I thought.

'*Namaskar*,' she said.

'*Namaste*,' I answered, waiting for Mustana to introduce us. He didn't.

The women were still coming. A plump young one came in through the next doorway with a little girl on her hip. Unfazed by our presence, she walked straight up to us, grinning. Then she lifted her shawl-covered arm and pinched my cheek. The little girl stared at me, her chocolate brown eyes made all the wider by their thick black rims of kajal. Several more dark-eyed children gaped at us from the corner, peering over one another's heads. Some ducked under other's armpits. Even inside the relative sanctuary of Mustana's house, we were still a spectacle.

I glanced up at Dave. His head was nearly touching the roof. The children were giggling. Then a third woman approached. With her filigree nose ring, dark lustrous hair and delicate features, she was extraordinarily beautiful. She had a baby strapped to her chest and was nursing it behind the sling. As she smiled at me her face lit up. I smiled back. For a while we just stood there, gazing at each other in mutual amazement.

'Namaste,' I said finally, my vocabulary almost exhausted.

'*Namaskar*,' she answered, clutching my hand.

Over by the hearth, the two women remaining had swiveled around to face us. They grinned at us toothlessly, their faces wreathed with deep wrinkles. Mustana's mother and aunt, perhaps? One held a dish of rice in her lap, picking out the stones. The other was plaiting a little girl's hair. Taking advantage of the lull, the other children tore off outside to spread the news.

It felt as though we'd blundered into a very private world. It didn't help that K S alias Mustana still hadn't introduced us to anyone. No-one spoke English. To be fair, our Hindi was pretty poor. That is, limited to Namaste and Shukriya and Do chai or whatever we were ordering. Numbers up to ten: ek, do teen, char, panj etcetera. There were no phrasebooks in Amritsar, although we later found a few in Delhi. No *Lonely Planets*. Back then, you learnt stuff from people on buses, or in the street.

Our host was nowhere to be seen. For the first time in hours, I began to relax. The women sat us down on the sofa. They oiled my hair and painted my eyes with kajal. They did Dave's eyes too.

Mustana's putative wife brought tea. We began to unwind.

Then K S burst through the entrance, flanked by a couple of men. More pressed through behind him. More still peered in from the porch outside.

'My brothers,' K S gestured vaguely.

Twenty brothers? Dave's look was skeptical.

'I am being the youngest,' said a tall, skinny fellow with buckteeth. His dark hair stood upright on his head in thick, crinkle-cut waves and his fine, thin mustache was curled at the tips like Inspector Poirot's. He looked nothing like Mustana.

The others were a motley assortment, some in turbans, some bare headed. They gaped and gazed wordlessly.

'Where are you coming from?' asked Youngest Brother. He rolled his head from side to side.

'Australia,' said Dave.

'Austrellia!' Youngest Brother grinned a buck-toothed grin. 'Many felicitations on your magnificent success in the cricket Test, yes?'

Dave smiled weakly. Once again, he'd failed this basic test of masculinity: he knew nothing about cricket.

'You are having this Donald Bradman, isn't it?'

'It most certainly is,' said Dave.

'You are following the cricket, yes?'

'No.'

'But Austrellia is playing world-class cricket, top-notch, isn't it?' urged Youngest Brother (it was 1978).

'I suppose so.'

Youngest Brother was becoming distressed.

'Good morning,' he said desperately, putting out his hand. 'I am having the name of Chandra.'

'Pleased to meet you, Chandra,' said Dave, shaking his hand.

'This is finish now!' K S announced with a peremptory clap. 'Time is getting on. We must be off again.'

Pardon? My headache screamed and hammered. What was K S aka Mustana talking about? What about our nap?

Dave rose to his feet. 'Can't you do something?' I implored. 'Talk to Mustana?' But Dave was not exactly comfortable here in this house full of women. He was hardly going to protest on my account. In desperation, I looked to the women. Perhaps they'd empathize with my distress, even intercede for me. But they failed to see it. Smiling graciously, they ushered us out the door.

'Please be coming now!' snapped K S, as we stumbled out behind him. 'We are becoming late, isn't it?'

To my great relief the crowd had subsided. People had gone back to their ordinary tasks. A few watched as we walked past, but they continued with what they were doing: hammering things, carrying pails of water, chopping wood. K S strode ahead of us, turning every now and then to insist we catch up, but never quite waiting for us. It was clear where we were in the pecking order. Who are the houseboys now? I could hear him thinking.

It struck me that our host's gait had changed. Down in Amritsar, he'd moved about silently, head bent, shoulders deferentially drooping. Now he was swaggering mightily, ape-armed, bandy-legged, with his chest thrust out like a baboon.

First port of call was his favorite chai shop. They were preparing special chai here, he informed us, according to his own original recipe. We stood outside. As earlier that morning, there were no seats inside. As K S flounced around, tossing off random comments to everyone he saw, we heard a mesmerizing sound. Tracking it to its source, 50 meters up the dusty main street, we found some youths lugging half a dozen drums onto a low platform. The drums were of different shapes and sizes; only later would I learn to distinguish the hand-beaten tabla and mridang from the dholak and madal, played with sticks. As we approached, the youths stopped tapping, dribbling, banging and testing and began to play. A small boy, younger than the others, picked up a pair of drumsticks and dribbled them across the tympanum. The older boys played with their hands. Using a seesaw motion, they rolled the drumskin with the ball of their palm then hit it with their fingertips. We stood and listened, transfixed by the complex rhythmic interplay. Within seconds dozens of onlookers had gathered around, swaying, jiving, tapping fingers on wrists, and all of them singing along.

I don't know what it was. Perhaps I was clapping. Perhaps Dave was shaking his pre-dreadlock dreadlocks. Out of nowhere K S came rushing over in like a small tornado. Bounding onto the platform he wrenched the drumsticks out of the child drummer's hands. We watched, aghast, as he smashed it down on the madal with such force that we expected it to burst apart. Prancing like a monkey, crouching like a kitten, springing up and down on rubber knees like a jack-in-the-box, K S drove everyone away – even the drummers. Eventually we were the only ones left. Then a man in a pillbox cap stepped up – the drum-master perhaps? – and told K S to hand over the drumsticks.

'*Tee chha*! *Tee chha*! *Chup raho*,' our host muttered, stepping down. Okay. Okay. Shut-up.

We were moved on up the road. We had places to go, people to be seen by.

For another 50 meters or so, things seemed deserted. Shopfronts were closed, palm trees bent lazily in front of porches. We were bathed, briefly, in mild winter sunlight. After all the excitement of the house, the walk was almost pleasurable. Shortly, we stumbled onto the explanation for all this tranquility. The main street emptied onto a large central square, blocked by bodies. K S paused to let us catch up. Then he grabbed Dave by the sleeve and pulled us forward. It was a national holiday, he explained, and everyone had come out to attend the local school's speech day.

Deeper and deeper into the crowd we went, K S tugging Dave's arm and me cleaving to Dave's slipstream. People barely noticed as we came up behind them, but word soon got out. Heads were turning like sunflowers to witness the unlikely convoy: small Indian man with a baboon-walk, tall white man with wild stormy hair, and a small, dark-haired woman, immodestly attired in trousers.

Finally, K S stopped. Up ahead we could see a high stage on which half a dozen officials were seated. Resplendent in a vermilion sari, a magnificent Indian woman was speaking in a loud, clear voice. As people stared at us, I fixed my eyes on her. Fifteen minutes passed. Twenty. Thirty. The sun was growing warm. We were still in jeans and jumpers. My headache jammered. There was no shade. The magnificent woman's speech ended to a sedate round of applause. Then another began, and another. The speeches were solemn and lengthy. Then came the presentations: bronze statuettes, silver

217

goblets, elaborate bouquets wilting in the sun, followed by the children's choir.

On and on the formalities went, while the sun rose to its zenith and receded to some indeterminate afternoon position. Dave began to nod off, standing upright. I keeled drunkenly as the afternoon sun whipped my eyeballs and crashed through my skull. Suddenly there was a sharp poke in my back. K S was clicking his fingers, summoning us to attention. Dave jerked awake.

'Come, come,' said K S, striding out again. The crowd parted to let him through, then closed in behind us, forcing us to follow him. Snot-nosed children reached out and touched Dave's clothing. Someone yanked his dreadlocks, chortling with mischief. An adult quickly cuffed the offender.

We'd reached the stage. Half a dozen functionaries gathered around, shaking hands with us earnestly and ushering us up the steps. Speaking into a microphone, a man turned towards us, raising his arm in a gesture of welcome. The audience clapped faintly, too awe-struck to respond. The man handed over the microphone. Clearly, we were required to do something; speak, croak, address the audience.

I stared out into a sea of faces. I hadn't realized how large a gathering this was until seeing it from the stage. Perhaps a thousand silk and cotton shawls billowed in the breeze like streamers or sailcloth. All waiting for the immodestly-attired white woman and the tall crazy white man to address them.

My heart knocked at my ribs. This nightmare had gone on long enough. It was time to wake, to wake up. I closed my eyes, opened them again. A thousand villagers still stared at me, waiting.

'They won't understand us,' I whispered to K S. It wasn't quite true. English had been part of the school curriculum since the Raj.

He dismissed me with a wave. 'Sing,' he said. 'You are having the Australian song.'

My headache raged and howled. I felt like I was about to faint.

'You're the singer,' said Dave, dropping back. I glared at him. This was no time for flattery.

Okay, I thought. Get through this. Sing something.

I took the microphone. Sing what, though? In my panic I couldn't think of a single song I knew. 'Twinkle Twinkle Little Star'? 'God Save the Queen'? I stood there, gaping like a fish.

It was Dave who came to my rescue. Taking the microphone from me, he improvised a tribute to Mustana.

'Ladies and gentlemen, friends, Romans and countrymen, I am hereby called upon to address this most auspicious gathering…'

The knocking in my heart eased. Dave was good at speeches, if a little flowery.

'…in order not to thank our extraordinarily kind host Mr K S Mustana,' I shot him a startled look, 'who has on this very day shown us the most appalling lack of hospitality…' I looked at him in horror, '…that we poor innocent travelers have ever had the misfortune to experience.

'And furthermore, who has foisted we unsuspecting travelers upon this poor unsuspecting community of yours with neither warning nor invitation. For this and many other disgraceful oversights we hereby proclaim the aforesaid to be the most execrable, most intolerable, most obnoxious little shit we have ever, in our 11 months of grueling travel, indeed in our entire lives, had the misery of encountering.'

It would not have taken much to push me over the edge and Dave's speech nearly did it. I dared not look at him. Instead, I clutched my stomach to stop myself cackling like a madwoman or screeching in terror. With baited breath, I waited for the penny to drop. Any moment now the enraged mob would surge forward to tear out our hearts and pulverize our bones.

Perhaps Dave was having the same thought.

'…and so, in conclusion,' he continued, reddening, 'I just want to thank our extraordinarily kind host Mr K S Mustana for his generosity in inviting my wife and myself to Your Beautiful Billage. I speak for us both when I say that we are deeply grateful to be experiencing the Indian hospitality. It has been a truly unforgettable privilege. Thank you all.'

We stumbled down from the stage amid voluminous applause. Dave was tight-lipped, trying to hold it all together. How was it possible? Had they not understood him? Whatever, we were more than glad. With every handshake from the waiting bevy of officials my pulse rate subsided and I began to breathe again.

We followed K S back out through the crowd. Thank Christ. Dave and I exchanged relieved looks. Perhaps now the worst was over. Could we go back to the house now, perhaps? Retire from the show-pony circuit? Take a long-awaited, hard-earned rest? Was it too much to ask?

But no, our Extraordinarily Kind Host had further plans for us. As we left the square the audience started following us, Pied Piper fashion. Children in their Sunday best put their hand out for money, curious old women pinched my face and arms. Young boys ridiculed Dave's height and punched him in the back before adroitly vanishing into the crowd.

It took some time to get back to K S's house. He hadn't quite got percussion out of his system. The drums were sitting idle in the middle of the road, the performers nowhere to be seen. Without a moment's hesitation K S mounted the low platform and grabbed the drumsticks. Raising his arms theatrically, he belted out a chaotic rhythm. With every hit my head exploded. Stop! Please. Someone wrap my head in cotton wool. A small crowd gathered, numbers swelling by the minute. The crowd pressed in until we were squashed up against the platform. K S took the opportunity to stand on tiptoe and peer down the front of my shirt, perhaps to imply that he and I were on intimate terms. Still reeling from his lucky escape with the speech, Dave chose not to react. Even I could see that manhood was not the issue here. Sleep, escape, survival – these were the things that mattered.

Back at the house I didn't even try to hide my pain. I had the worst of all migraines. Black shapes were blotting out my vision. My ears rang and my skull was in splinters. I could no more smile politely and pretend it wasn't happening than conjure up a spaceship. K S was suddenly Mustana again – all compassion and concern. He installed me on his own marital bed – the only double bed in the house, as far as we could ascertain from glimpsing the narrow bunks in the other rooms – then stayed on to watch me 'rest', despite Dave's assurances that his presence was not required. It became a battle of wills: Mustana morphing back into K S, ogling me as I lay down, fully dressed, and refusing to leave us alone, versus my boyfriend. Dave was a gentle guy but his chagrin had been steadily building and he was ready to explode. Eventually, K S left, only to return a few minutes later; did I need my sleeping bag?

No thanks. Some Vicks Vaporub? (True, the very same, made in India.) No thanks. An extra pillow? No thank you. Some clean pyjamas to slip into? For Christ's sake, Dave said forcefully, no!

K S slunk away.

Frantically, we schemed. It was almost four o'clock. Our chances of catching a bus out of town at this hour weren't good, even if I could handle the ordeal of another journey. Services might have finished for the day. Even if we did find a bus, or score a lift with a passing truck, it would be hours before we arrived at a decent-sized town. It'd be hard to find accommodation in a strange place after dark, Dave pointed out. I agreed with him. The prospect of spending the night in a cold and distant bus station had little appeal against the option of staying right there, where I could slide into a delicious semi-comatose state.

Besides, the women of K S's family had been so nice to us. I thought of Mustana's kind-faced wife and her trays of sweet spicy chai. I thought of the plump young mother who foisted steaming samosas on us, and the beautiful young woman who'd held my hand and smiled. How could I be so cruel as to hurt them? They would not understand that we were running from their odious male relative, not them.

In the end we resolved to leave in the morning, at the crack of dawn.

Three pills and a short nap later I was feeling slightly better. Dave was snoring but jerked awake as soon as I moved. We went out into the main room. The women were sitting around, combing one another's hair, talking. Several were chopping food in the kitchen. We told them we were going for a walk. They didn't try to stop us.

Outside, we practically ran – away from the houses, plunging into the countryside. This was Mustana's realm: extensive fields of wheat and mung beans, a few lean sheep grazing the verges. We walked to the edge of a high spur. A river surrounded it on three sides. Steep rice terraces layered the descent like contour lines on a map. The opposite banks rose steeply, framed by high blue interlocking bluffs which formed a horseshoe around the valley. Higher still, another ridge of mountains, frosted white like jagged lace, formed a vertical horizon. Nothing lay flat in this country, it seemed.

We found a trail down and crossed the river at the bottom. We might have kept going, mesmerized by those mountains, had we not met a woman who insisted we come back to her house for chai. As the sun set behind the peaks, her five barefoot children alternately scurried away from then returned to beam at us from behind her pyjamas, their teeth as white as Himalayan snow.

V

We got back to K S's house around dusk. To our great relief, there was still no sign of him. Perhaps he'd run away, we fantasized gleefully. Without him, the household seemed less tense, and far more interesting. Names began to emerge. Although we had barely a word of language in common, the beautiful woman and I managed to have a hilarious conversation, gesturing at Dave, at her baby, and drawing pictures of our lives with our hands and lots of absurd facial gestures. I found out that her name was Sita and she was married to Rahul, one of Mustana's brothers. For the first time in 18 hours, I felt myself relax. I tried to find out how many women lived there. There didn't seem to be enough beds for them all. The answer was unclear. Some lived next door, same house. Or different house, here, they indicated, confusing us. They kept saying yes, no matter what we asked them.

The light was dimming now. Shutters were closed, hurricane lamps lit. The women began to play with me, stroking my hair and plaiting it down my back, the way they wore it. They painted black kajal around my eyes and thumbed a circular red bindi on my forehead. A red streak along the middle part of my hair completed the picture. Now I looked like a married woman, they smiled approvingly. The fake wedding ring wasn't quite enough.

Someone conceived the idea of outlining Dave's eyes with kajal again. The earlier application had gotten smudged from his oratorical labors up on stage. They painted his forehead too. With his red and white-striated brow, his unkempt hair and ragged clothes, he looked even more like an Indian sadhu. Shanti, the plump, married woman with the dark-eyed daughter, presented me with a pair of pyjamas. She wanted to swap them for my jeans. Sorrowfully, I declined. I'd given away my spare pair in Kabul – these were all I had. No matter, they laughed, sprinkling me with sandalwood oil. I was their sister.

VI

At around nine o'clock K S returned, drunk. As he came through the front door, other men pressed in behind him, until at least 20 had squeezed into the room. Such a big family. So many 'brothers' and most of them no less drunk than Mustana. Mustana's wife, Lakshmi, along with her daughters-in-law,

Shanti and Sita, brought out lashings of food, then disappeared into the kitchen.

We were starving. K S told us to please be eating our fill. Over a communal meal of chapattis, rice and dhal he introduced us to his clan: his father, his three younger brothers, various uncles, cousins and members of Lakshmi's family. Chandra, the buck-toothed man we'd met earlier, was actually Lakshmi's younger brother, which helped explain the lack of resemblance. He asked us how indeed we were enjoying the repast.

'How indeed?' said Dave, but Chandra missed the irony.

The women came out to clear the plates and were gone again within seconds. Over in the corner, K S and some of his brothers were taking swigs from an unlabeled liquor bottle.

'We will now be having the entertainment!' pronounced Chandra, standing in for his brother-in-law in as master-of-ceremonies. Drums were brought out and a flute of some kind; a hookah and spittoon. I tried not to wince as pots were rattled, kettles banged. 'I am being Michael Jagger!' bellowed Chandra, holding a cucumber up to his mouth. 'Jumping Jack Flash'.

No-one else seemed to recognize the song. Failing to get a response from us, he stuck the cucumber on his groin and simulated masturbation. Now he got a reaction: the men laughed and smacked their thighs, leering and hoiking globs of phlegm into the spittoon. Several times we looked meaningfully at our host, who'd promised us an early night, but he avoided our eyes. Not knowing where we were meant to sleep, we had no choice but to stay and watch the unfolding spectacle.

The night lumbered on. The cacophony grew louder and more

dysphonic. Sadly, the women had vanished for good. Only the burping, spitting, gyrating, shouting men were left. Dave was exhausted beyond belief, his eyelids drooping, yawning continuously. Only chivalry kept him awake. I found out later he'd been imagining the worst. He feared I'd be sex trafficked, while he was sold off into the slave trade to star in a snuff movie, or some such grim fate. Had he been alone he'd have happily succumbed to sleep, and to hell with the consequences, but with me there he couldn't. While Dave wrestled with his conscience, not to mention encroaching somnolence, I entered a state of delirium. Exhausted beyond belief, strung out beyond all measure, I could have happily slept in a pigpen.

Long after midnight, we declared a stay of proceedings. We'd given up waiting for K S's cue. We were going to bed now.

Everyone stopped talking. All eyes were on us.

'You are in need of repose, isn't it?' asked K S, materializing out of the shadows.

Well yes.

'And so, where is it that are you thinking of having your sleep?'

What was he talking about? Hadn't he promised us a bed for the night?

'In the same bed, or different beds?' K S prompted.

Did we have a choice? We could hardly kick him out of his marital bed again. His wife was probably there already.

'No, please. Any beds will do. Whatever you've got.'

'So, it is two beds you are wanting, isn't it?'

The beds we'd seen were pretty narrow. Two might be a good idea, we thought. 'Well, if you can spare them,' said Dave. 'Yes.'

'Really? You are wanting two beds?' K S raised his eyebrows, incredulous. 'But you are man and wife, isn't it?'

It was too hard to explain our two-year de facto union at this hour. 'Yes. Absolutely, man and wife,' we lied, hallucinating sofas. Whatever, please, just let us lie down.

'Then you will not be wanting two beds. Or is that you are wanting separate rooms?'

Was this a thing in India? we wondered. Double beds for married couples, as long as they slept in separate rooms? It seemed like a contradiction in terms but I was too tired to think about it.

'So, you are wanting separate rooms then?'

'Oh no,' I gasped, the implications suddenly dawning on me. I did not want to sleep apart from Dave, not in this houseful of men. 'The same room, thank you. Two beds, one room.'

Spike Milligan chimed in. 'So, you are wanting two beds in your room,' he pointed at me, 'and two beds in his room?' he pointed at Dave.

'No,' said Dave irritably. 'My wife and I want to sleep in the same room.'

'But in two beds, isn't it?'

Dave shrugged. The conversation was exasperating beyond words.

'But excuse me,' Spike Milligan aka Chandra persevered, 'if you are having two beds then you cannot be wanting to sleep together, isn't it? So, you can be having two separate rooms.'

I clutched Dave's arm. No! I mouthed at him, imagining stealthy advances in the middle of the night, K S and his caricature of a brother padding around our solitary, separate beds. I'd not hear a thing as they quietly slit Dave's throat in the next room. Likewise, when Mustana and his fellows set upon me my cries for help would go unheard.

Ever the pragmatist, Dave had a more mundane interpretation. 'Two beds might be overstretching the family's resources,' he whispered. 'K S is just too embarrassed to say so.'

'What we want,' said Dave, turning back to our hosts, 'is one room and one bed. Two beds if you can spare them. Whatever's available.'

'Aha!' Spike Milligan let out a whoop of delight, slapped his knee. 'So, you are wanting to sleep together, isn't it? In the same bed.'

Desperately, we appealed to K S for help, who grinned his encouragement. Then several 'brothers' slipped out through a door. Maybe, I dared to hope, they were going home? Maybe the rest would follow? Five minutes later the brothers were back, dragging a double bed behind them. With great fanfare, they set it up right in the center of the room.

'This is your bed!' Chandra announced. 'Hereupon you may be taking your repose tonight.' All I could see were his huge buckteeth. 'Isn't it?'

A dozen gaping, leering faces turned our way, thrilled at the prospect of witnessing the nocturnal intimacies of two weird Westerners.

My head was spinning. Dave's face had turned a peculiar shade of green. Sleep, hissed a voice inside our heads, sleep.

VII

At dawn I woke up, stiff and sore. The household was silent. I glanced around at the slumped forms of Mustana's neighbors and kinsmen, lying with legs draped over one another, faces squashed against walls, bed-legs, bodies. Others lay spread-eagled on their backs, snoring loudly. Half a dozen were skewed across the bed, limbs flopped across one another's mouths or stomachs or backsides. Chandra was snoring through his buckteeth, Mustana's head was buried beneath a blanket, his legs sticking out, and another 'brother' drooled into a puddle on the floor. Dave and I had slept sitting up, with our backs against the wall. Our feet throbbed painfully inside our boots and we stank of sweat, stale vomit and bootleg whisky.

I woke Dave. We made no noise, packing up. Miraculously, our departure was witnessed by no-one and sometime later that day, we managed to flag down a passing bus.

CHAPTER 15

F*CK I LOVE VALiUM!

Kol Dimond

I was trekking east to west across the Indonesian archipelago from East Timor to Bali as cheaply as possible when suddenly my trip began to get a little weird!

Instead of a taxi or hire car I decided to mix it with the locals and get a microlet. These minibuses are ten-seaters officially but try telling that to 23 of the dudes precariously hanging at all angles to the outside frame of the bus.

As the thermo reached 40 degrees in the shade, I thought my luck was in when only five people were on the bus waiting to take the 40-kilometer trip south and my ball space, which I have become fully accustomed to in the west, was still intact. After 30 minutes of sitting motionless the bus turned around and started going in the opposite direction. I yelled out in my best tetun (local dialect) *'Iha nebe sentina.'* To my amazement the bus stopped next to a big roadside ditch and the driver was pointing to me to get off. I stood my ground until an old man across from me yelled in bad English 'You pisser.'

This wigged me out and I got off the bus pronto and walked hastily across the road into the shade to collect my thoughts as the bus drove off without me! Upon close examination of my language book I soon realized, instead of asking the driver where the bus is going, I had asked him 'Where is the toilet?' Thus, the confusion…I felt a right twat.

Anyway 15 minutes later I was on bus number two with equal ball space and enhanced optimism for the journey ahead, an optimism which lasted all of about three minutes. It started off with the old man and his chickens, soon followed by the 150 kilograms of rice supplies thrown on the roof, which made the exhaust drag along the road. I soon realized the nightmare had only just begun as the bamboo, the mangoes, the local nutter shouting to herself the whole journey and finally the school excursion all seemed quite happy to somehow place themselves on me and settle in for the road trip.

This scenario of course did nothing to quell my anxiety attacks and after a little game of personal Twister I somehow managed to maneuver my nostrils so that they got close to one of only two open windows on the bus. Finally, the bus left the terminal and a sort of paralytic calm oozed through my body as a small breeze flowed into my lungs. It was now that the hidden 4K sound system kicked in like the fucking Blitz next to my ear drum; 4000 watts of distorted, max volume, East Timorese Gangnam style with a twist that nobody except this Aussie doofer seemed to give a shit about. Amazing how compliant these people were. No-one even twitched. Business as usual as the bus now crawled along at about 35 kilometers an hour towards the hills with its arse dragging along behind it.

Two and a half hours later, the 40-kilometer journey was almost complete. A toddler was asleep on my neck and his dad on my shoulder. My foot was numb, but hey I got the full cultural experience I was looking for. As we came into town the engine sort of fell out the bottom of the vehicle, and me, the chicken herder and a weird assortment of human beings pushed the deflated vehicle the last hundred yards or so. I was in Gleno ten minutes later drinking a coke as the bus seemingly made a miracle recovery, turned around, hooted its horn and headed back on the return journey.

Hindsight is a wonderful thing. After the bus trip, I was convinced things could not get any worse. How wrong I was. Two days after the bus trip I wrote the next part of my travel blog feeling like I was lucky to still be in one piece. Let me explain.

I fucking love valium. And I don't say that lightly. I have never been a big val user but on this occasion it saved my skin, and I'm thankful for that. I had just spent more than 33 hours in very intense travel mode. Leaving East Timor and heading west to Kupang you really get to see the devastation the Indonesians inflicted. They tore all the roads up that they had initially built, heading west, back into what is now West Timor's capital, Kupang.

The three-hour trip to the border was horrible. Mega road building was taking place all along the journey as they tried to reconnect themselves to what is basically the rest of the world. As soon as you cross the Indo border the roads turn into smooth bitumen and you feel like you have entered a different system completely. It's a painful reminder of the war and Indonesia's part in it.

Two bizarre things happened that day. Firstly, in the middle of the night I rose too quickly from my top bunk in the dorm to pull my sheet over my feet and put my head straight into the ceiling fan. It cut the bridge of my nose and bled all night. Once again, I felt like a right twat. Secondly, as we crossed the Indo border and the third set of fucking Indonesian Gestapo guards wanted to search my bags and question my forays into East Timor, one young soldier saw my music CDs and he asked me what was on them.

I told him 'Techno,' and he said 'DJ music?' And I said yep, and then right out of the blue the fucker said 'Minimal?' and I was like, what the fuck, and said, 'This one is more progressive,' and he said 'Nice.' So I asked him if he wanted one and told him it was a mix that I had made back in Australia, and the dude stopped searching through my bags and let me through. How cool was that? Some nutter in jackboots and a Hitleresque mo digging some phat beats. I had to chuckle at the thought of him getting home and busting out some moves.

So, I finally get to Kupang after 13 hours and there was a local ferry going over to Flores the following morning and I thought, fuck it I'm outta here, and booked a ticket. The ferry was packed to the rafters with all walks of Indonesian life. After a three-hour delayed departure, it was on, and what a hideous trip it turned out to be. It was 37 degrees, 80 per cent humidity and there were no windows that opened.

I was okay till about three in the morning when the anxiety kicked in. Too many old men staring at me sweating my cods off and not being overly friendly. I couldn't sleep anywhere and in the middle of the night all the crazies came out. I was losing the plot and started hyperventilating as I struggled to find my comfort zone. I was the only whitey on the ferry and it turned out to be an 18-hour endurance test.

Once I realized I was in trouble I ripped the lid off the valium that I had brought from Oz and double dipped. OMG…how good are those little fuckers? It took my anxiety away and gave me my swagger and confidence back, which I heavily rely on whilst traveling. By the time I got off that ferry I was completely emotionally and physically drained, and as any avid South-East Asian traveler knows, it was unlikely to be the last time.

So, there I was in Flores looking for the Hobbit caves, where bones were discovered a couple of years earlier, which had got the locals pretty revved up. I told them we had midgets back in Oz but they did not seem overly impressed with my humor.

I would spend a day or two there getting my strength back then head over to Komodo National Park to look at the dragons, which are magnificent creatures and add another dimension to this incredibly vast and complex country.

As a side note, Chelsea were one nil up at Sunderland. They love their footy there. At times the similarities between nations are very simple. Over but not out.

CHAPTER 16

IN THE HEAT OF THE MOMENT

Simon Williams

Sometimes while traveling you see things you thought you'd never get to see, sometimes you see things you never want to see again.

I'll be totally upfront about it, I have never harbored a desire to set foot in India. Even though there are people who swear by their experience in that country. They say that India changes them as a person, that it opens their eyes to appreciating life. This quote by Keith Bellows of the National Geographic Society is one such example: 'There are some parts of the world that, once visited, get into your heart and won't let go. For me, India is such a place.' Good on you Keith. I am sorry I do not share your undying love for the subcontinent mate, I would honestly rather go on an excursion through war-ravaged northern Nigeria wearing a T-shirt stenciled with, 'Boko Haram sucks dick'.

As fate would have it, while I was planning a 'thank the fucking universe I am still alive' birthday world tour, after a near death experience on the Pacific Coast Highway near Malibu, I stupidly made a comment to my travel agent that I had always wanted a photo in front of the Taj Mahal. Rather than him understanding that I was implying I had always wanted a photo in front of the Taj Mahal except it is in India so I'd rather pass, he took that as affirmative to add India to my list of destinations. My travel agent is also one of my best mates and drinking partners, so despite his egregious error, I will have to forgive him. So, this is how I find myself on a plane bound for India, to satisfy a random, intoxicated wish to get a snapshot of myself standing in front of the Taj Mahal, and nothing more. Unlike most, I honor my drunken rants to the letter. Preferably I would be in and out of the country as fast as I could without seeing any poverty, catching malaria, or having to watch a cricket game in 45-degree heat and humidity. If I can squeeze in a ride on top of an overcrowded train then I will consider that a bonus.

My flight from Paris lands into New Delhi at the ungodly hour of 2 am. I had bought myself a brand-new edition of *Let's Go India,* which I had intended to thoroughly read on the flight but instead spent my time more productively chatting up one of the Air France stewardesses. For a few seconds before touchdown I scanned the accommodation section for the city and saw three or four hostels costing the equivalent of US$1 a night. Trains to Agra were 50 cents. I may not enjoy the next three days but at least my stopover in India was only likely to cost me ten dollars. Immigration at Indira Gandhi International was a breeze, there is very little reason for anyone to be denied entry into India. You can arrive without any money to support yourself and they will let you walk on in. They country already has 500 million people who don't have money to support themselves, what is one more.

I enter the arrival lounge and the first thing that I need to do before I think about where am I going to sleep tonight, and how will I get there, is find a toilet. Before I can take a step in the direction of the little illuminated figure representing a male body I am besieged by three hawkers for taxi services.

'Do you need a taxi, sir?' Asks the first.

'Do you need a taxi, sir?' Asks the second.

'Do you need a taxi, sir?' Asks the third.

It was comparable to being in character in the nursery rhyme about the three little pigs. Then the big bad wolf told the three Indian hawkers that he would eat them all for dinner, but they kept on aggressively pestering the big bad wolf to utilize their transport services until the big bad wolf went insane and shot himself.

I firmly told them to just let me go take a crap first and then I would happily come and discuss terms with them. Apparently in India that doesn't even qualify as a brush off. The three men follow me into the bathroom, all the while asking me if I need a taxi. I open the door to a toilet stall and drag my backpack inside, the three men have the never-say-die tenacity to follow me into the stall. In what is truly a remarkable design feature of the toilet stalls at the New Delhi airport, they are five meters long. This is more than enough room for two pieces of luggage as well as five or six hawkers. They are more than willing to bunch up into the available space to enable them to continue propositioning someone's attention for their services.

I looked at them, 'Really fellas? You want to stand there while I take a dump?'

'Do you need a taxi, sir?' They ask in unison. I'm guessing that my good friend Keith Bellows didn't have this type of welcome party when he came to India. Or maybe he had just a lone hawker intrude on him while he did his ablutions, and the sparks from their encounter are what endears the country to him so much.

In all honesty, it doesn't bother me in the least, so I drop my pants and sit down on the commode. Unlike some writers who are wordsmiths in their descriptive style of personal interactions, I have developed my art form to be extremely vague regarding my encounters with locals in the countries I have traveled to. All due to the fact that one day I knew I would be writing a story about the time that three little Indians followed me into a toilet cubicle at the airport on my arrival into New Delhi. I've always intended to spare my readers the graphic details of those 15 minutes.

Job done, I wash my hands thoroughly in the basin. Then I wash them again. I felt I had to be clean enough for all four of us. By this time, I am down to just two admirers as the third, bless his heart, just didn't have the stomach for hanging around during the crucial late rounds when I was struggling.

'Do you need a taxi, sir?' They ask again.

'Guys, you have been asking me the same bloody question for the last 20 minutes. I think we have established I need a bloody taxi. Next one who asks me if I need one will be out of the running, okay?'

Almost by instinct the first hawker smiles and gushes, 'Do you need a taxi, sir?'

My voice becomes terse. 'Right you, piss off. You failed. I hope you don't have enough money to pay for gas to make it home tonight because of your stupidity.' I turn to the other hawker, 'Okay mate, I want to go to a hostel.' I pull out my *Let's Go* and am just about to show him my desired budget accommodation in the Indian capital when the driver grabs my bags.

'I know a very good place sir,' he says.

'It had better be cheap. I don't want to pay too much. This is India, you people should be paying me to be here.'

'Very good sir. It is a very nice place.'

'Is it cheap?' I persist.

'Very nice sir. Very good price. For you very good price.' He continues babbling.

'Mate, I don't think you have any idea just how cheap I am. Even by your standards I'm sure I'm still cheaper.'

I follow him outside and to the parking area; I have to, he has my backpack. The cut-throat nature of Indian transportation means that if he left me waiting while he went and collected the car it is likely that someone else would have swooped in and convinced me to leave with them. That is sound logic, I have little loyalty to taxi drivers at the best of times and certainly not in New Delhi at 3 am. By swiping my bag and running away with it he has guaranteed that the 15 minutes he spent scrutinizing my 'giving birth face' was time well spent.

We walk through a sea of identical, indistinguishable white vehicles until we reach his. His car is the classic Indian automobile, a Hindustan Ambassador. This style of vehicle was originally modeled after the Morris Oxford car series made by the British Motors Corporation in 1956. Remarkably, in the 55-year history of its production in India the model did not undergo a single upgrade. I guess when they make them that good to start with why would you want to change? We drive out of the airport and into the sprawling metropolis housing 14 million people.

The car stops outside a dimly-lit strip mall. The only business with a light on is a small travel agency next to a dry cleaner. This is not the cheap, derelict hostel I was expecting. My driver urges me to go inside. Now things are extremely dodgy. I am exhausted, I am confused, but I really have no choice. I am alone and really at the mercy of my driver. This is always the great decision to be made when considering traveling the world alone. How will you feel wandering into a strange country and the time comes to be mugged and left to die? I've given this a lot of thought. I believe there is tons more cachet in cashing in all my chips while surrounded by Islamic militants in Nigeria screaming, 'Come at me you pussies,' than being taken out back of a New Delhi dry cleaner and bludgeoned to death with a sitar.

I stumble inside the travel agency where I am greeted by a well-fed Indian man sitting behind a desk with a phone.

'Good morning to you sir,' he bursts out, 'How can I be of service?'

'What am I doing here? I wanted to go to a hostel.'

'Very good sir. Let me help you out. I can get you in a very nice hotel. How much are you looking to spend?' He asks cheerfully.

'One dollar.'

'No sir, seriously.' He responds.

'I am being serious. One dollar. There are some hostels here that only cost $1 a night.'

'I do not know of anywhere that cheap sir.'

I open my *Let's Go* and show him the page where the hostels are listed. His mind kicks in to overtime as he contemplates how he can overcome my steely determination to pay $1 for accommodation.

'They are closed now.'

'Why? You are open. What type of travel agency is open at 3.30 am?'

'Let me call them.' He picks up his phone and dials a number, I suspect he is just dialing any number he wants, then follows with a two-second conversation before he hangs up. 'They are full.'

'What? Are you sure they are full?' I question.

'They said they were.'

'Then the next one,' I insist. 'Here, let me be the one to use the phone.'

He slaps my hand away, rapidly dials again and this time the conversation is even shorter. That hostel has no vacancy either, apparently. Dammit, I must have arrived at the very height of the travel season for budget conscious travelers visiting the Third World. We argue back and forth for about an hour over letting me be the one who dials the phone. At some stage the fatigue of my long flight and early arrival, coupled with my exhaustion of being the patsy of a well-orchestrated tourist shake down, takes full effect. Sensing that my guard has dropped, the man behind the desk launches into full-on sales pressure. Let him make it easier on me, didn't I want to go to sleep? Where would I like to go in India? What glorious sights did I want to see?

'I just wanted a bloody photo in front of the bloody Taj Mahal!' I explain.

'Oh, very good. I am sure that will make your trip to India very memorable.'

'Nope. Having three guys watch me take a shit has already fulfilled that aspect.'

He pulls out a calculator and starts punching in numbers as if he is actually making a calculation. Three nights luxurious hotel accommodation including private vehicle transportation from New Delhi to the Taj Mahal in Agra. Would I like to add in a return trip via the pink city of Jaipur? I have never heard of Jaipur before. As fascinating as the lure of driving an extra three and a half hours to see a city filled with buildings bedecked in my least favorite color would be, I had arranged to meet the Air France stewardess at her hotel on my last night for drinks. Cold gin and tonics with an airline stewardess, or visit an obscure, rose-tinted city baking under the hot Indian sun. Even accounting for the fact that she was French, that decision takes me all of half a millisecond to make.

I suspect there are standard procedures involved with bartering over prices for goods and services during daylight hours that would customarily still apply at 4.30 am. Normally there is some parry and thrust between parties, a little give here, a little coming down on price there. When I was told it would cost me $220 for an entire package to cover my three days stay, I am sure there might have been some wiggle room if I wanted to try and fight. But I just went, 'fuck it' and tossed him my credit card. He could have even raised the price on me after that and it would not have made a difference. End of the first round and so far, it was a one-sided fight. India 1, Simon 0.

It is 5 am before my driver delivers me to what I was informed would be a four-star rated hotel that is a member of a hotel chain that I will be staying in. I suspect that each hotel in the company had been awarded a half star and the enterprising CEO of the company had simply added those ratings all together. Now I don't mind staying in a flea bag, cockroach infested hell pit that has stains on the sheets and no running water, as long as I am only paying one dollar for the privilege. Then I at least expect it. Thank God, the locally made, tiny air conditioner is operable, because even at this early hour the humidity is stifling. I've spent time wearing fleece pyjamas in a Swedish sauna that was on fire and been more comfortable than I was in this hotel room.

My sleep, or lack thereof, only lasts until the sun comes up and the wall unit AC doesn't have the manpower to keep up with the full-frontal assault of the heat. How is this possible? This is early May, so in my mind still in the Northern Hemisphere spring. However, that is before I learn that India's seasons are slightly different than anywhere else in the world. Winter on the subcontinent runs December to February and then the country goes straight into summer. That season is over by June and then starts monsoon season. Three months of continuous downpours is followed by the post-monsoon season, because the Indians couldn't come up with a better description for it, then they are back to winter again.

So even though I had left Paris wearing a pair of jeans, I should have had my G-string thong easily accessible in my hand luggage to change into once I arrived in New Delhi, to better handle the heat. The temperature I was experiencing was like nothing else I had known, even back in my own sunburnt country. I now better understood why Hindu, the predominant religion of India, didn't believe in an everlasting hell. Because there is at least a post-monsoon season to break up the torment of living there.

Unable to be comfortable in my room, I peak my head downstairs to see if anyone is in the lobby. I had given thought to running from the travel agency Gestapo and making my own way to a youth hostel. Daring, I know. That is how spooked I was with the whole situation of being held captive at their mercy; I was willing to bail on my pre-paid stay. I didn't have any idea where I was in the city, whether they were coming back to get me, or if a photo at the Taj was worth all this aggravation. I scan the entrance to the hotel and there is my driver standing guard at the front door waiting for me. Holy crap, I wasn't expecting that. It was a little freaky. Or maybe I was misreading the entire Indian approach to customer service. This guy was so devoted to having me not waste a single second of my time exploring the sights and diversity of his wonderful country that he was willing to camp out in my hotel to make sure he was always available when I needed him. So, he is either incredibly cognizant to be at my beck and call, or he is a psycho.

'Good morning sir, can I help you with your bag?' he asks.

'Do I have a choice?'

First stop for the day is my driver's relation's rug store. The only thing positive I can glean about being made to go rug shopping at 8 am is that the shop is air conditioned, but that still doesn't excuse my driver from forcing me to do it. In my opinion, if I have seen one rug I have seen them all and I remember seeing a rug when I was five. There is of course enormous craft involved in the multi-generational development of the talent to produce such embraided masterpieces. However, if Indian culture had spent one tenth of the time needed to advance their skills in rug making and instead applied that effort to developing air-cooling technology then the country might have become a more enjoyable place to visit.

The three-hour drive to Agra starts on a flat boring plain, blessed with soul-sucking heat highlighted by a horizon of shimmering distortion that makes the desolation of the Simpson Desert landscape look inviting. It continues and ends the same way. Every God from every world religion has forsaken this stretch of highway. I must beg my driver to stop every 20 minutes at roadside stalls so that I can chug an ice cold, refreshing beverage to prevent my body from going into hypovolemic shock from dehydration. They say that the joy of travel is in the journey not in the destination. The people that have the nerve to say this have never been here. I would give the bowels of Hades two stars on TripAdvisor compared to the state of Uttar Pradesh. While the north of India is graced with the majesty of the Himalayan range of mountains, peaks that uplift spirits and which force men to dig deep into their reserves of determination to overcome their individual mortality, the moron who built the Taj Mahal didn't decide to build it there. That genius chose Agra, the holding tank of the septic system that makes up the majority of the Indian peninsula.

My driver pulls over to the side of the never-ending road at a random point and a man jumps in the front passenger seat. This must be how fly-by-night companies masquerading as tourism operators handle their abduction of tourists in India – they outsource it. How ironic. My irrational fears are laid to rest when he is introduced as my personal guide for my visit to the Taj. Wow, my own private chaperone, how pointless. I don't need someone to point out the Taj Mahal for me, I have seen it in pictures often enough. Any relevant history of the place I will simply make up, it always makes it more interesting. Now, did I already pay for this guy to follow me around? Can someone please remove this item off the bill and give me a refund? I only plan on getting my photo taken, leaving, then finding a bar with a ceiling fan where I will chug a yard glass filled with cold water.

We arrive at the wall behind which is the Taj Mahal. The story behind the building of the translucent marble edifice is truly a love story for the ages. Commissioned by Shah Jahan in 1631, it was constructed to honor the memory of his wife Mumtaz Mahal, who succumbed to the pains of childbirth of their fourteenth rug rat. She wasn't his only wife; he had seven. Most men after the arrival of their fourteenth child are in the urologist's office asking to be snipped and worrying about how they will finance the next grocery bill. Most men after dealing with the hysterics of one wife aren't in the mood to go about marrying six more. But not our good mate Jahan, he was nothing if not a gutsy bugger. For the grand design to console his broken heart, he planned to spend the money in his children's university savings accounts to not only throw up a glistening mausoleum to honor his lifeless Persian princess, but possibly also to construct an even larger, black marble one across the river for himself. Unfortunately, this was his undoing. Jahan's third son, Aurangzeb, angry that his father would no longer pay for his liberal arts degree at Agra Community College, imprisoned him in Fort Agra until his death. Legend has it that he was given a cell with a small window overlooking the construction site of the Taj Mahal so that he could still try and spit on the grave of the wife that produced the son that betrayed him.

I wander the expansive grounds of the mausoleum in absolute awe that Shah Jahan could find any laborers willing to work at any price in this heat. Over 1000 elephants were employed to transport materials from all over the Mughal empire to Agra, while 20,000 artisans toiled to decorate the structure. Stories abound of his ruthlessness in inspiring workers to bring his vision to fruition. He would cut off the arms and hands of workers so that they could never again build a more beautiful building. This is perhaps where the Hindu concept of a temporary hell and reincarnation was born. If the workers knew they would be staying in hell forever they wouldn't have been so scared to go on strike and be executed. They would have been happy to accept they were going to a cooler place permanently. The concept of being reincarnated acts as a deterrent to work stoppages, as it eliminates the thought that there is any true escape from the purgatory of the subcontinent. It is much like my experiences when forced to go into an air-conditioned rug shop at the urging of my driver. It is a moment of relief, followed by inconsolable anguish, knowing that my time in that hell will be only short-lived before I return to the pea soup outside.

The true beauty of the Taj Mahal is that the inside marble surface is decorated in a lapidary of precious and semiprecious gemstones. Artisans cut elaborately designed decorative elements, such as flowers, fruits and vines, into the solid rock wall. These are then inlaid with the gemstones that have been perfectly shaped to fit without any bumps in the surface of the wall. Time-consuming stuff. Other notable features of the complex are the 35-meter-high marble dome that surmounts the tomb, and a 200 meter lap pool in the front yard that is much too shallow to swim in. At the time

I am here, the pool had been drained to sterilize it after a child had dropped his chocolate bar into the water.

At the far end of the Mughal garden is the Great Gate, which is decorated with enough pink to satisfy any regrets I might have had of bypassing a chance to visit Jaipur. Standing beside it, I decide that this is the place. This is where I will take my photo. My tour guide/ remora fish eagerly indicates that he will take the picture. I am very hesitant, apart from the fact that this man's limited knowledge of the Taj Mahal hasn't exactly overwhelmed me with curiosity, I am not about to trust him with taking possibly the most important photograph of my entire life. About the only thing he has told me of interest was that when Princess Diana visited they closed the complex so that she could experience it alone. No wonder the poor woman was so lonely and depressed. Who wouldn't be if they didn't experience one of the crowning jewels of antiquity without rubbing shoulders with a million unwashed Indians.

'Do you know how meaningful this photo is to me?' I ask him.

'I am very good at taking photographs. Very good.'

'Very good doesn't cut it with this photo mate. You need to be Rembrandt.'

I hand him my camera. It has taken me 12 hours of suffering to get to this momentous point, Krishna help him if he screws this up. Already today I have recycled 14 gallons of water through my body, through drinking and sweat, without needing to go to the bathroom. During my life, I have found that most people have not the faintest idea of how to take a photograph. I am not talking aperture settings and light composition, I mean that if they are taking a photo of Big Ben that bloody Big Ben is actually in the photograph. If my guide takes a photo of me and behind me is only blue sky I'll be mad enough to piss on his mother's grave, although I currently can't retain enough fluid in my body to produce urine.

The year is 1998, digital pictures are not yet a thing, photography is still nitrate film and one-hour processing. There is no way I will know the outcome of his clicking the shutter until three weeks later when I am in Australia. No way I can kick his arse if some random Indian decides to photobomb me without me being aware and spoils the prize I have been seeking. He lines me up, has me shuffle to my left a little, then presses his finger.

'Take some more,' I urge him.

'No need sir. It is a magnificent photo, very good indeed.'

I breathe an uneasy sigh of forced relief. If you can't trust some random man that your psychotic Indian driver picks up on the side of the road in the middle of nowhere, who can you trust?

CHAPTER 17

MOUNTAINS AND UNICORNS

William Dalton

1 October 2017

If the Island of Lombok were a woman, she would be breathtakingly beautiful, compassionately kind, yet chilling ruthless. She'd, smiling, welcome you in, then desert, or worse still, murder you, without hesitation.

Here are my three dates with Lombok. The first time I set foot on Lombok was a week ago in nothing but swimming shorts and an oxygen mask, en route by makeshift ambulance, to the nearest decompression chamber, Mataram Hospital. Yep, got the bends from diving. As we sped on the winding road to the ER I acknowledged, 'This is a weird introduction to Lombok.'

The second interaction with the Island was two days later. Happy and successfully decompressed back on Gili Air Island, I was sipping a coffee looking at Lombok while pondering the odds of successfully swimming to her sandy shores, only a couple of miles across the channel. Everyone advised against it, but her golden beach was beckoning, 'come on over, you know you want to'.

If Bondi's Dori Miller can do a double crossing of the English Channel, then surely this should be easy. Plan: swim across, get a boat back. After battling a stronger than expected rip current I finally emerged on Lombok to see boats everywhere, yet oddly, the place was deserted, all but for ten, six-year-old boys who enthusiastically welcomed me. They stared, prodded and poked at me as if I was an alien emerging from a spacecraft. 'Hey, you little punks, where are your parents?' Ultimately, in the absence of an adult boat driver, I had no choice but to swim back to Gili.

My third encounter with Lombok was supposed to be a pit stop. I was on the fast boat to Bali, then to the airport to jet out. We left Gili Air Island and arrived 15 minutes later at Lombok harbor to pick up others passengers bound for Bali, when we were abruptly told to get off the boat because it had 'broken down'.

It appeared to be running just fine to me. The next boat was promised a few hours later. I stood on the jetty with my luggage in the midday sun, what the fuck is my next move?

I walked up the dock, to an area that looked like a scene from the movie, *Hotel Rwanda* with hundreds of shoeless, dark skinned people hustling in the rubble. Then on the left, a Japanese man in his mid-twenties was lying face up in the scorching sun, wearing only his swimming trunks and flippers as a Westerner violently performed CPR on his lifeless body.

That guy is dead, 100 per cent. Nobody seemed to care. In the West the police would cordon off the area, there'd be a helicopter in the sky, emergency vehicles at the scene. Here, nothing.

What a shit show.

I walk by the dead man. Nothing else to do. I enter the dodgy looking harbor cafe, a cramped, nest-like environment with dozens of locals swarming. Sitting there completely out of place is a stunning English blonde in her mid-twenties. In Notting Hill, we'd barely acknowledge each other, here it was like meeting a long-lost friend. El planned to climb Mt Rinjani, Indonesia's second highest peak, and was waiting for a shuttle bus to take her to the induction meeting for her three-day trek. I'd seen the summit from Gili Air Island.

After an hour of encouragement from El and a two-hour car ride, I'm at the induction meeting surrounded by a dozen Westerners in their early-to-mid-twenties. I'm not an ageist but I'm the oldest there by at least two decades.

The meeting was led by Eddie, an Indonesian dwarf, who assumed that El and I were a couple. Yes, literally a dwarf. Don't worry, I just google checked, it's okay to refer to a little person as a dwarf, just not a midget. El and I had to explain, 'No Eddie, separate rooms.'

Day one. The next day we set out at 8 am to the park entrance and trekked for seven hours to our campsite at the rim of the volcano. After the second hour, it dawned on me that I'd probably made a terrible mistake. Up until now, I've been successful in living in denial. Yeah sure, I am 48, but I can do everything I did when I was 22…right?

Wrong.

By the time we reached the campsite, I was hammered. Yes, I kept up with the 20-year-olds, but just. When we arrived, my one-man tent was perched on the side of the mountain, set up by the porters, cloud cover beneath us. Fantasies of an evening tryst with El were replaced with, 'hope I get off this mountain alive'.

Overnight the temperature dropped and by midnight I couldn't figure what was most uncomfortable, the rocks digging into my hips from the mattresses-less tent floor, or the cold.

Day two. It didn't matter because at 1.30 am we were up preparing for our 2 am departure to the summit. An estimated three hours up and two hours down. Not for me. It took me four hours up, and four hours down. An hour and a half up the mountain I was both admiring the beauty of the starry sky and panting for oxygen. The air was thin and the 20-year-olds had all raced ahead, while our guide was forced to stay back and keep an eye on me.

I could see lights at the top, and imagined we were only 30 minutes away. 'No, it's two and half hours at his pace,' the guide said. The last one kilometer to the peak was essentially deep gravel. You take three steps forward and then slide back two steps. Frustrating as hell.

On the way up, members of other teams were strewn around the mountainside like litter. Some were just sitting there crying. They'd given up. Dizzy and nauseous, images of the dead Japanese diver passed my mind like clouds.

Why the fuck am I doing this again? I told the guide. I am done, let's go back down. Then I contemplated the significance of the cliché metaphor – failed to climb to the mountain top. Couldn't live with that, had to keep going.

On finally arriving at the summit I wasn't happy, I wasn't sad, I felt late for work. The 20-year-olds were already on their way back down. My quad muscles were shattered. It hurt more going down than up. While the rest of my crew were eating breakfast and playing

20 questions, I limped into camp eight hours after we departed and was handed a plate of white toast and jam, cardboard would have had more nutrition, and then informed we were leaving in 30 minutes for the three-hour descent to the lake at the volcano floor.

WTF? I just arrived!

The way to the crater floor consisted of descending almost vertical faces. Our guide was now carrying my backpack, annihilating any vestiges of self-pride and any positive impression El may have had of me. True to form I rolled in last. Twelve hours of climbing, hiking, trekking was done. The scenery from the lake was mind-blowing. To balance the harsh and ruthless personality of Lombok, were several soothing and reassuring thermal pools heated by the volcano, only a few minutes' walk from our camp. I sat in one of the pools, the temperature of a very hot bath, and contemplated the many faces of this island and the nine-hour trek out the following day. If Lombok had a personality, she'd be clinically described as a psychopath with sociopathic tendencies, with a penchant towards random acts of kindness; that is, of course, when she's not drowning Asians. The hot pools reflected her softer, kinder side.

Day three. At 3.30 am the next day I stumbled out of the tent like a Yeti, feet bruised, bloodied toenails and gravel rash on hands from falls. I put on the same clothes, had tea, and by 4 am we were on our way.

We were told that the vans were picking everyone up from our departure headquarters at 2.30 pm so that gave us over ten hours to get back. Once again, the 20-year-olds left me for dead.

Ten hours of hiking later, at 2 pm I emerged out of the gates of the national park, with a 30-minute walk back to our departure station.

I felt high, exhausted, lightheaded and hungry.

My body began taking deep breaths, that merged into sobs – I can't believe it, I'm fucking crying – then managed to get a grip. This was way harder than expected.

A man on a motorbike from our base camp cruised up the road shouting my name, he pulled up alongside and insisted I get on the back because I'd miss the van transfers to port that were leaving in 15 minutes.

I entered the camp on the back of the bike to cheers. Would have preferred to have walked in, rather than submit myself to further humiliation, being rescued; after all, I was only on the bike for two minutes. The rest of my crew were all showered and in clean clothes, happily piling into the minivans that were now all waiting for me. Fuck! I hate this rushing shit.

It was only a few minutes before various people started to gently, and not so gently, prod me to hurry up and get into the van.

Understandably since they'd all just done the same climb, it must have been difficult to empathize with what I was feeling. I told them to go, opting to get my own car.

When they left, there was a beautiful silence, just me and Eddie, the smiling dwarf sitting across from each other. The dwarf gave me some toast, and I pulled out my Vegemite jar from the luggage and offered him some. Upon tasting, he scrunched up his face like he'd bitten into a lemon – to which we both laughed.

CHAPTER 18

THAI SURPRISE

Matt Towner

Serendipity is a splendid thing when we are lucky enough to experience it; those one in a million moments that even 25 years later offer a sense of wonder and a gratitude. Anyone who has read some of my short stories, published in the various books of Travelers' Tales, will know that I spent the decadent decade of the 1990s traveling the world as a gem dealer. In the days before the internet, we would regularly line up in busy Third World post offices to send postcards to loved ones. Just to let them know that we were in fact still alive.

The Bangkok branch of the world of mail was always a busy one. Not just love letters, but big boxes of all sorts of bargains were sent daily to all sorts of destinations. Mail could be received there if you were game enough to take that risk. If you could afford it, a new invention called a fax was available where letters could be sent and received in the same day, for a hefty price.

I sent my very first gemstone from that post office in an elaborate plan to quadruple my money on a beautiful blue sapphire, bought in Thailand, home of the best of that beautiful stone anywhere in the world. It was posted to London, where the legendary Lady Di had created a global sensation with her elegant engagement ring. This was her entrance to the royal family. My stunning sapphire did not make as grand an entrance to the old country.

After days then weeks of it not arriving at the home of my friend in Highbury, I bit the bullet and hoped it did not backfire. I phoned English Customs explaining that I had posted an expensive gift from Bangkok to Britain but it had not arrived. The cockney wide boy on the other end of the line took all of my details with a bit of banter. 'Diamond Geezer Pucker Pony' and all that in it. My name, my sending address, my receiving address, the contents, all of which I was scared to say, but it had to be said. If it had just disappeared, I had lost thousands of dollars, which I could not afford. There was a shocked silence over the phone; I could feel it more than hear it. 'Matt Towner…Matt from the Highbury Barn?'

Before ending up in Thailand flat broke and desperate, I had spent a summer working in a classic old pub in North London. 'It's Mikey, Johnny's bruvva'.

Really, what were the chances, the ringleader of a bunch of lads who drank in that pub every night, as people do in the UK would take my call? I had no idea he even worked for Customs and then there was the fact that he answered my call from a public phone in the mailroom in Bangkok. He went from official to underhanded in a heartbeat. 'Where do you want me to send it?'

The stone had been seized and serious duties were due if it was to enter England at all. But Mikey could redirect it, he explained, and it would then be the next country's Customs who would either accept or deny it, but hopefully for me it would go straight through, as I had first hoped.

Switzerland was my next best bet and I had a couple of great mates there I knew I could trust. Mikey was magic as I fumbled through my pocket-sized address book with the black leather cover but well-worn pages. He filled me in on all the latest news from the boys around the old bar. I got off the phone still in shock. But the story got stranger, in a worldly way. I ended up not making it to Switzerland but the sapphire made it all right. Straight through customs and waited with my friends, as I smuggled stones back and forth from Asia to Athens that summer.

I was back on my feet and flying through the air, so a sapphire in Switzerland was the last thing I needed, but it was a nostalgic notion. I had my amigos in the Alps send the stone to my folks all the way back to Australia. Again, it flew fine and as a bump in a birthday card and it awaited my return. That gorgeous gem beat me home by about two years and had been from Thailand to England to Switzerland to Australia; a round-the-world ticket, which many of my mates would have loved.

I decided that stone should never be sold and I never did. It traveled the world with me for another five years. I proposed marriage with that stone but as most modern women do, my bride to be wanted diamonds. And who could blame her, diamonds are a girl's best friends and De Beers are the best marketers of anything on the planet. Did you know that amethyst is rarer than diamonds, but no other stone has the sales pitch and product placement of those beauties? So, I had the sapphire, my first ever stone, made in to a rose gold ring of detailed design for myself. Unfortunately, our wedding never happened which was heart-breaking at the time but the ring rocked on and I wore it for another 15 years before losing it in a waterfall in the Blue Mountains. Where else would a blue sapphire go to retire after 20 years of travel from the Bangkok Post Office.

...

Back in that fine but dirty and dangerous city, and in that very post office... we were up the back of the busy post office scribbling short notes on the backs of funny photos. Our travel partner, business broker, comrade and comedian was in the long line awaiting process for postage of consignments and cards to both clients and to colleagues, friends and family. Behind him in line, from over his shoulder, a luckily longer-legged man noticed overseas names and addresses. He hesitantly made mention that he actually knew a few of those people. Carlos the Portuguese replied in his unique but never subtle way, 'Well if you know these guys, you must know that guy,' pointing to me at the back of the room, where sound still traveled, especially the sound of Carlos.

Now if you have read any of my stories, you will also know that the names have been changed to protect the guilty unless otherwise confirmed. Not that we ever did anything wrong...so, let's call the gorgeous girl beside me with the pen in her hand and the world at her feet, Lola. And let's name the tall, surfy superhero looking towards us, Stu. This second of many moments of serendipity in my life must be made clear. If Stu had not noticed those names, which he knew, the chances of us meeting in that ram-packed room full of comings and goings, with hundreds of hustlers and bustlers, was as slim as a stamp. We had no idea that any of us were there at that time. By there, I mean anywhere in the world. In Australia we had been the best of friends and every card Lola and I addressed would have been to the same set of soulmates that Stu would have sent his to.

Carlos was silenced, which just never happened, by the rejoicing reunion between three long lost friends, far from home and even further from who we had once been. To paint you a picture, a postcard in that post office, Carlos looks like he sounds. A pocket rocket Latin lover who had traveled the world for 20 years buying and selling stones. As confident a character as I have ever met, a man's man who feared nothing and showed it, every minute of every day. His look was that of Che Guevara with pizazz. Stu was always cool calm and collected, from our school days to present day. At black tie balls when we were mere boys not yet men, rather than the standard tuxedo, Stu would wear sterling silver collar clips and leather string to match his leather jacket and pointed boots. He was always immaculate but in a messy way that only the cool can do. Even in board shorts and T-shirt he stood out. He looked like he was about the catch the next wave, even in the city.

Asia for me always brought a goatee with it. I had learned very quickly that if I walked the streets clean shaven, even covered in jewelry and long hair, announcing to the world that I was stepping out, I would still be pestered by every second street seller to buy everything from Rolex copies to tuktuk rides. But grow a goatee, that half beard of bikers borrowed from wild westerns, and no-one stopped me, and often side streets would open so that I could walk on by.

Last but never least, Lola. One of the Thai street sellers we supplied with gemstones and jewelry, in exchange for baht and banter, said it best, when she smiled, the whole world smiled with her. We had been first loves at the age of 15 and then in our twenties were traveling the world with Carlos the Portuguese, a market-trading magnate.

Our paths are all so different again now and Lola is happily married with two beautiful boys growing into men. I am also magically married – which surprised not only myself, but many others – after 45 years of finding my way. It took a long time and an amazing woman, who has helped me get to this point. Putting pen to paper typing away, remembering and rejoicing, relearning and retelling. I hope Lola likes this story and her man and her boys see that twinkle in her eye, which I know that they love, because in that moment in that madhouse of mail, we all shone like diamonds. And Stu was flying out the very next morning, so we had him for one night only!

I always aim to avoid cliché whenever possible, as cheesy as I am, but that was 'One Night in Bangkok'. As much as I never liked the song, I loved that night. Fantastic friendships are one of the most heart-warming feelings on earth. That night we were on fire! Celebrations started immediately and in our usual fashion, with a streetside banquet, offering every Thai food delight and drink we liked. The sign of true friends is when you may not have spoken for years but when you do meet again, it's just like yesterday. You can pick up a conversation mid-sentence as if you had just ducked to the bar. It just took a wee while.

We were so on a roll that Carlos rolled over, went to bed and left us to it. But we had only just begun. We hardly took a breath between us, only to eat and drink. More so we devoured our friendships and embraced the excitement of the new journeys that we were undertaking and overtaking. From private schools and prom dresses to a life on the road in some crazy convertible with no rear mirrors, just a mirror ball and a looking glass. Full of life we were. One night in Bangkok you can see it all, the good the bad and a ladyboy show. The seedy side of the city was never our thing but one thing led to another and bad ideas come good. We ventured from Khao San to Patpong, in search of Miss Adventure, just for a laugh.

The infamous ping-pong shows were something I thought that I would never see. We still didn't see it really. We were so engrossed in our own adventures and the connection of our conversations that the bizarre burlesque performances happening all around us were more wallpaper than features. Darts flew through the air and razor blades were announced as pythons hissed and people kissed but we were in our own world.

We could not believe our luck that our paths had crossed. It had only been weeks earlier that Lola and I had been at the full moon party on Ko Pha Ngan, selling stones in the markets on the beach, when another friend from our old school days literally cruised on by. Not on a boat but with a swagger which was more of a saunter. Let's call him Ryan.

Ryan was that guy at school who made everybody laugh from the principal to the preschool toddlers. He took pride in his work and he joked like it was his job. Like Stu he made messy look suave. But he took silly to a whole new level from a very young age. He did it well, very well. He was larger than life, so much so that this world was not big enough for him. As soon as we started to drink, as 16-year-old schoolboys, he would drink more than anyone else. By university days, when an iconic Australian business mogul suggested learning to smoke, pot was mostly on offer and Ryan could smoke more than anyone else. But he could always hold his cool and continue his comedy. No matter what we did he did more and more.

When he happened upon heroin, we all took a collective gasp and we worried about him as a group. As all good friends should. But there is not much anyone can do without the will of the one. And when that one has such a wonderfully wicked but whale-sized will, it is hard to stop, and Thailand is no place to come. Another of our school-days darlings had seen that first-hand. Her first night in Bangkok, only early twenties in age, as we all were, was a night similar to ours, but she was befriended by a charismatic stranger, but hardened by experience. Perhaps he had been there too long. That very night, her first night, after dinner and drinks and bright lights and fairytales, he offered her a safe bed to sleep. But as she awoke, he never did. This was a fate we feared for Ryan, an amazing man we all loved.

As we saved him in our minds, over shots and pseudos, in the seedy bars of Sukumvit, the sun was well and truly up. The all-night pharmacies offered us sunglasses and salvation from hangovers, which would have hurt. But we were bulletproof now, even from ping-pong balls. Stu suddenly remembered like a lightbulb going off, his flight…that hurt. Tuktuks and taxis, checked out and changed, he bid us farewell. Leaving as abruptly as he arrived, like he just needed a stamp. As Lola and I lay thinking, dreaming of sleeping, suddenly we were re-awakened by a knock and a laugh. 'Missed my plane…breakfast anyone.'

Years later we were all reunited again. Not just those of us in this story who took the old school tie to the road less traveled. Many more of us, in fact most of the misfits and mismatched from those private school years, came to pay their respects. Ryan had been one of the forerunners in running away and only a few of us followed. Not so much to his extremes, none of us could. But we followed that dream of a life on the road rather than suits and ties. No picket fence, no nine-to-five, and if we did, it was just for a while. How much we wished he had been with us that night. To know how much we cared and that we were scared. But he knew everything and through everything he was always an amazing man in my eyes, the hero of this story, even though he was not there.

I remember the phone call that morning and how much it took me back to Thailand. I will never forget him because his story is a script I am still writing today. A story of friendships as strong as that night, but this time four mates from school called in to battle, as a body lay lifeless. Laid out before him was a set of gemstone runes, which Lola and I had created as a business born from those Bangkok days. Runes are an ancient tarot, a reading of one's future through symbols and choice. Much like life is all about symbols and choice. Ryan had chosen Berkana, the rune of new beginnings.

Serendipity comes at the strangest of times, from Bangkok to Brisbane, from sapphires to school reunions. Some months after Ryan's passing, I had a deep and meaningful with a dear friend of all of us from those rebellious days, who said that 'Hey if anyone wants to leave this life why not go the way of Ryan.' He romanticized, as many do, that purple haze which I have been lucky enough to never know. I have even been lucky enough not to have an addictive personality. I have been able to take or leave anything. My only addictions today are Facebook and Netflix, which in my opinion are two of the most addictive of drugs. But way before these inventions and only months after Ryan left the building, our friend I will call Dean, who had humanized heroin to me as a philosophical footbridge, back flipped completely and hung himself.

So, my offer of this story is not just to say please seize the moments, especially when the magic happens. Not just to embrace the beauty of your friendships and the joys of travel, the art of adventure. But if you are experiencing crazy sh*t in Asia, or anywhere, or are just back from the dead and battling those demons in your bedroom alone, please phone a friend. If you know someone struggling, then please call him or her. That may just make all the difference, it could be that moment of serendipity, the occurrence and development of events by chance in a happy and beneficial way. Feel free to call me anytime as I continue to write that script.

CONTRIBUTING WRITERS

Kerrie Atherton

Originally from Sydney, Kerrie Atherton now lives on the Sunshine Coast, Queensland. She is the founder and host of 'Stories of HOPE' Australia, a successful monthly event that brings hope to people all over the Sunshine Coast through the stories of real people, overcoming real challenges. Having overcome much adversity in her own life, she now teaches people how to find hope through motivational speaking, counseling, school-based and parent-targeted programs, along with many other events. Kerrie has been married for 30 years and has two amazing, adult children with two small granddaughters. She has a passion for travel and fashion.

In her work as an experienced addiction and teenage/family crisis counselor, Kerrie sees the damaging effects of dangerous choices and many lives left in ruins. Because of this, she has a desire to reach not only young people and parents with prevention and early intervention programs, but also to reach the Australian community as a whole. Her mottos of 'don't do life alone', and 'together is better', are present in everything she does.

Warren Boggs

Warren is 45-year-old Australian who became a paraplegic in 2000 after falling down a waterfall in the mountains of northern

Thailand. He then worked at Chulalongkorn University for two years in Bangkok and later spent six or so years teaching high school science in Ghana and South Africa. Like many Aussies, he has made many trips to Asia.

Warren lives in a small town in the south-west of Western Australia. As a paraplegic, he loves pointing out the positive things that 'wheelies' can do.

Bronwyn Clifton

The household Bronwyn grew up in was often pretty chaotic, with six children under one roof in Melbourne. She escaped the bedlam by reading stories – telling herself stories to go to sleep; and it's something she still does.

In the early nineties after completing a Bachelor of Education, she traveled overseas with a friend, backpacking through Europe and the United Kingdom. On her way home, she visited Thailand on her own. This experience, then more recently going to Vietnam, inspired 'Confessions of A Massage Junkie'.

An avid reader, Bronwyn has been writing in one form or another for many years.

Bronwyn lives with her husband and 16-year-old son near Black Swamp, Victoria.

William Dalton

Will Dalton is a teacher and spiritual counselor. As a teenager in Australia, Will left school to crew racing yachts. By age 20, he was an ambitious real-estate mogul on the rise. He learned to meditate in order to conquer the business market – or so he thought. Will quickly fell in love with Eastern philosophy and his life soon took a different turn. For the last two decades, Will has traveled the globe teaching yoga and meditation to all kinds of people, of every age, race, and creed. He also authored the book, *A little story about the biggest thing that ever happened,* as an exercise of the heart, to express all he has realized about the universal nature of spirit and the mechanics of creation, and to contemplate what happens when humans forget their essential nature.

Kol Dimond

Kol Dimond is simply taking up too much room: a freelance open-source agitator bent on change.

Born into an awkward time and place back in 1962, this male version of a skanky 'ho' won't rest until the world flips upside down and equity and love replace greed and hate as the governing forces in a new world order.

A creative nuisance who judges success by those who have little ambition and desire for wealth, many songs and words have littered his low-impact, high-mileage journey across the planet. Seeking adventure and meaning at all ports, and along the way finding love children and friendship. The future is not what it used to be but the past will always catch up with you.

Love and revolutionary vibes.

Piers Fisher-Pollard

Piers Fisher-Pollard loves writing just about anything on any surface and has been experimenting with his craft since he was a tween, more years ago than he'd care to mention. His poetry, articles and short stories have been published around the world and he holds a Master of Arts in Creative Writing from UTS in Sydney, Australia.

Piers presently lives in Byron Bay with 11 cats, is searching for his missing canary and attempting to write his first full-length novel on a double-length toilet paper roll with a fountain pen. It's refillable.

Leila Hall

Leilah Hall is someone who loves to travel, and sees the funny side of most things. The ordinary entertains her immensely and she loves to bring humor into almost everything's – 'cos most things are really entertaining when you have the right lens.

She has lived in the US, South Africa, India and Thailand, and now calls Australia home. She works in finance which will help her fund her writing career in her retirement.

Ian Harris

Ian Harris was born in the United Kingdom and migrated to Australia at the age of ten. He studied medicine at the University of New South Wales and hasn't stopped traveling since, living at various times in the United States, New Zealand, Indonesia and Singapore. His main aim now is bucket list travel. In the last few years he has ticked off Burning Man, Superbowl, Cannes film festival, Sundance film festival, Bluesfest, Glastonbury, Desert Trip, Coachella and Summer Solstice Festival in Iceland. So far Ian has traveled to 58 countries but still has another 137 to go.

Ian now lives in Byron Bay, Australia, and as well as traveling, his interests include languages (he speaks French, Spanish, Indonesian and Malay), surfing and snowsports.

Megan Jennaway

Megan Jennaway grew up in an era when writers honed their craft by being anything but a writer. Accordingly, she has been a waitress, barmaid, shop assistant, radio announcer, organic farmer and academic before turning to write more seriously. Along the way she has published a number of short stories, one winning The Canberra Times National Short Story Competition Schools Section. In 1977, aged 19, she and her boyfriend threw caution — and their university studies — to the winds to do the legendary Overland route backwards. Their travels took them from London to Sydney via Turkey, Iran, Afghanistan, Pakistan, India, Nepal and Thailand — an experience out of which one of her two stories in this volume, 'The Indian Hospitality', was born.

Her cannily chosen subsequent career as an anthropologist provided further opportunities to travel, enabling her to live in Indonesia for almost two years, and to spend shorter periods working in India, Timor Leste, Vietnam and Solomon Islands. Before quitting academia for a writer's life in the Byron Bay hinterland, she was a Postdoctoral Fellow in Creative Writing at Queensland University of Technology. After this, in keeping with her penchant for doing thing backwards, she gained her Masters in Creative Writing at the University of Queensland. Now, when she and her partner are not traveling, planting trees or fighting off alien weed attacks, she works on her current novel.

Feather Kibby

Feather Kibby began her traveling life at 18, where she ventured off, on her own, to a small town in the Sacred Valley in Peru (without a clue what she was doing) to teach English in a tiny school in the Andes. This experience taught her not only how to survive without hot water for three months, and how to eat guinea pig, but started her never-ending, life-long journey and goal to step foot, explore, involve and dance the streets on every corner of the globe.

Since then she has been to 52 countries, across every continent (okay, depends how picky you want to be because she HAS NOT been to Antarctica) and traveled extensively throughout (her favorite) Australia. Her experiences have enriched her soul, created many lifelong friends all over the world, and most of all have forged enough stories to last a lifetime.

She has taught in schools in Peru, Turkey, Thailand, Hawaii and Alice Springs, as well as living in Berlin for what was probably the craziest summer of her life.

She graduated from Creative Writing at Melbourne University and is about to graduate from an Advanced Diploma of Steiner Education and Masters of Teaching respectively. She has a true belief that the education that Steiner schools provide enhances children to their capabilities of everything creative.

Feather's true passion is in writing, and she is currently working on a variety of children's stories and a novel *2013*, all based on her travels. She currently lives (in the best house) in Melbourne.

J 'Momo' Mordant

J 'Momo' Mordant, also known as Momo Mercurious, was captivated by comics, fantasy art and mythical literature. Somehow, fortunately, he managed to bring that into his later life by donning the mantle of a merchant adventurer, a global trader, a treasure hunter, a gypsy. He spent nearly 15 years traveling all over the world, enchanted by various tribal cultures and their shamanic traditions, while accumulating near-death experiences. It was a unique window of adventure before the leisure industry took to the skies and guide books greased the rails, where 'getting lost' revealed hidden gems.

Momo discovered international cowboy entrepreneurship which allowed him to wing a living on the road, without returning to 'civilization'. He 'worked' from busking and clowning to dealing antiques, clothing and gemstones, and loved to hunt for unusual minerals, often exploring deep underground in exotic, dangerous locations and then developed a passion for hand-carving stones and forging metals to create unusual jewelry and sculptures.

He continues to fulfill childhood fantasies of navigating hidden realms, under the sea and beneath the earth, and traveling paths less trodden around this magical azure precious rock. It's elemental, archetypal, ancient, artistic and totally alive!

Rock on!

Emily Saunders

Emily Saunders grew up in Tasmania with an unrelenting curiosity about what was round the next corner. As soon as she was old enough she left Tassie shores to explore this mystery properly. However, as we all know, what's behind the next corner is another corner. This led Emily to do a lot of searching all over Australia and around the world. Luckily, she found a partner in crime who loved to do the same, and they traveled to a lot of amazing places together. Emily writes a travel blog Twin Travelling about life on the road with her young twin daughters, and is currently writing a book about her three years in Israel. Emily now lives in Melbourne with her husband and children, happy in the knowledge that the world is still filled with undiscovered corners.

Matt Towner

Matt Towner graduated from university in Brisbane, Australia in 1989. Two days after his 21st birthday, he flew to San Diego to play rugby. That decision was always meant to be a life changer, but how much so, never could have been expected, especially for a boy from the bush who went to a primary school of only 20 children then a boarding school of 1000 boys. Matt played one season of rugby for San Diego and traveled most of America, but that was just the beginning.

Matt flew on to England where he planned to play rugby, but a nightclub changed his life and he traveled the world creating dance parties and as a 'gem dealing gypsy'. This is the title of his first book and the start of Traveller's Tales. Matt's website www.travellerstaleswriters.com is an online publishing house that allows travelers of all types to share their stories and have them published in books of short stories. These stories change people's lives, sometimes just as much for the readers as they did for the writers.

When Matt started traveling, the internet was unheard of and jewelers all over the world needed gypsies like Matt to bring them gems like diamonds and rubies, sapphires and pearls. Nearly every country in the world has a stone which no other country has, so for a capitalist hippie as Matt was at the time, it was his international passport to hedonistic heaven. These days, those same jewelers, as with any business today, can just Google for what they want, so times have certainly changed. Matt's upcoming book *Gem Dealing Gypsy* (www.gemdealinggypsy.com) offers you all of the insights and adventures of those crazy days.

A modern gypsy today can literally travel the world with a laptop and a mobile phone and make a living – if you know how. Matt has previously published a number of short stories including: 'The Pocket Book Guide to Byron Bay', 'The Gemstone Book of Runes', 'Crystal Carvings', 'Opal Magic', 'Rasta Roo', 'Bris Vegas' and 'Positive Investments'.

Simon Williams

Born in Townsville, Queensland, Simon now lives in Miami, Florida. He always wanted to see the world and still harbors a strong desire to visit Cambodia, Ceylon, and Leningrad, but is buggered if he can find where they are on a map. He has spent half his life having to tell Americans that he grew up near Sydney, as most of them have no idea that Australia has another city.

He found out how much he enjoyed writing when his 10th grade English teacher told him that he was lazy, so he wrote a 25-page story for his next essay just to annoy him. His sense of humor was developed over eight years of boarding school. As a way of both evading having the crap beaten out of him, while also dealing with being a smart boy who sat at the back of the class but who couldn't see the board because he refused to wear his glasses.

His favorite pastime is trolling his mates on Facebook and taking the piss out of them. He has only been unfriended twice, on both occasions by his wife.

First published in 2018 by New Holland Publishers
London • Sydney • Auckland

131-151 Great Titchfield Street, London WIW 5BB, United Kingdom
1/66 Gibbes Street, Chatswood, NSW, 2067, Australia
5/39 Woodside Ave, Northcote, Auckland, 0627, New Zealand

newhollandpublishers.com
Copyright © 2018 New Holland Publishers
Copyright © 2018 in text: Authors credited in text

A record of this book is held at the British Library and the National Library of
Australia.

ISBN 9781742572390

Group Managing Director: Fiona Schultz
Publisher: Alan Whiticker
Project Editor: Liz Hardy
Designer: Catherine Meachen
Production Director: James Mills-Hicks
Printer: Hang Tai Printing Company Limited

10 9 8 7 6 5 4 3 2 1

Keep up with New Holland Publishers on Facebook
facebook.com/NewHollandPublishers

US $19.99
UK £12.99